THE UNLIMITED AUTHORITY OF THE BELIEVER

Nothing Is Impossible

Pastor Mark and Anne Spitsbergen

TABLE OF CONTENTS

Foreword

Pastors Mark and Anne Spitsbergen "Belieiving for the Impossible" in Kathmandu, Nepal.

The Lord in His loving kindness and grace toward us has allowed us to do things in the nation of Nepal that no other ministry has done. In 2008, through the power that is in the name of Jesus Christ, we were allowed by God to hold the first crusade in the National Stadium of the kingdom of Hinduism. During those meetings we saw thousands of Hindus come to the saving knowledge of Jesus. God did many signs and wonders and a great number of people were healed of their diseases. On the last day of the crusade, when we looked up and saw the stadium filled with people, all we could do was stand in awe of what God is doing in the nations that have been held back from the gospel for so many generations.

We were asked to come to Nepal in 2011 to do Pastors and Leaders conferences in three different locations: Kathmandu in

Pastors and Leaders Conference, Kathmandu, Nepal.

Central Nepal; Bharan in Eastern Nepal and Dhanghadi in Western Nepal. The Holy Spirit laid this message upon my heart to share with the leaders of that nation. Afterwards, I committed to take my sermon notes and put them in a booklet form to be translated into Nepali. We are so blessed and privileged that we have been allowed by the Holy Spirit to participate with the advancement of the kingdom of God in the great nation of Nepal.

Pastors Mark and Anne Spitsbergen

Pastor Mark with his interpreter Ball Shiva, the leader of the Bible College, in the National Stadium in Kathmandu, Nepal.

Introduction

"Arise oh gates and lift up your heads everlasting doors, and the King of glory shall come in. Who is this King of Glory? The Lord strong and mighty, the Lord mighty in battle. Arise oh gates and lift up your heads everlasting doors, and the King of glory shall come in. Who is this King of glory? The Lord of hosts: He is the King of glory, Selah."

Psalm 24:7-10

A king is given the authority to bring all the power that resides within his kingdom to bear. If attacked by an invading army, the word of his authority mobilizes all of his defenses. If there is a need for conquest, everything under the king's dominion must arise at his request. Now we have been given such authority in our inheritance with the King of Kings that we may go everywhere and preach the gospel of the kingdom. We are priests and kings, the ambassadors of Christ who now stand in His place for all the world to see. We must preach the gospel like Jesus preached it if we are going to do what Father wills. "This gospel of the kingdom must be preached as a witness to all nations" with the power and authority of God, not men. We must arise and shine for our light has come. It is the light of Jesus and His ministry. This gospel of the kingdom that must be preached as a witness to all nations can only be defined by the ministry of Jesus.

God Almighty became the Living Word so that we could understand by example exactly what we are to do. The Word, Christ Jesus, came and displayed the unlimited power and authority of the kingdom through the gospel that He preached. It is this gospel that He has also commissioned us to preach as His co-laborers. It is a gospel of authority and power that we have been entrusted with to set men free from the tyranny of Satan. If we are going to follow Jesus, then we must accept the authority that has been given and do what God commands: proclaim liberty to the captives and the opening of the prison doors to them that are bound. Can you imagine a person who is given the job of a policeman, but refuses to believe that he has authority to tell people what to do? He has the uniform and the badge and is given an assignment, but is unable to enforce the law because he does not feel he has the right. His duty goes unaccomplished and thieves and criminals take over because the one with authority does not execute his job.

Unless we function in the authority of Christ we cannot be the witnesses that God desires or the people that Christ described. When Jesus was baptized in the Holy Ghost he began to reveal the kingdom of God with an unlimited authority. Then when He arose from the dead all authority in Heaven and Earth was given to Him. It is this unlimited authority of the exalted King of kings that He has given to those who will believe. The unlimited authority of the believer is revealed through: the authority of the kingdom of God, the authority of the Word of God, the authority of the Holy Spirit, the authority of the name of Jesus, the authority of the blood of Jesus, the authority of sonship and the authority of mountain-moving faith.

If we fail to recognize and believe the authority that has been given to us, then all of the fullness of God's glory and the life and ministry of Jesus will never be seen as it should. The thief that has come to steal, kill and destroy will go unstopped by those who were commissioned to destroy his works. The world that dwells in the chaos of darkness will not see the full radiant beams of the glorious light of the gospel unless we will believe! If the life and authority of the resurrected Jesus is to be seen, then someone must be a witness. Will you allow God to make you a witness unto Jesus and His resurrection? Will you believe that your glory has come, and stand up and begin to shine?

Hindus came to Jesus by the multitudes.

God has given us the ability to move in a realm of the Spirit where "nothing is impossible." He has given us every dimension of His power, might and strength. The most difficult part is our willingness to believe that all Heaven now backs us. God has freely given us this unimaginable blessing and gift – the life and authority of Christ! If we are going to grow and develop into the fullness of the ministry of Jesus, there must be a complete surrender and consecration to His will. We must give ourselves over entirely to the mentorship of the Holy Spirit who will lead us and guide us. The Holy Spirit will teach us how to do the works of Jesus just like He did them. He will train us in all the conduct and manner of His life. Through the training and guidance of the Spirit, the power of God will flow through us with the demonstration of great wonders and miracles; every yoke will be broken and every criminal of hell stopped!

We would be making a big mistake if we failed to look at the opposition that we face. Satan's chief enemy is the anointing that destroys his work and makes his power ineffectual. Just as he set out to kill Jesus before He could mature, he would also destroy or neutralize anyone that would walk in God's anointing. All the hosts of hell are devoted to stopping the yoke-breaking power of the anointing and working of the Holy Spirit through the saints. Satan will put up every hindrance possible and persecute the anointing to destroy it in every way that he can. We must realize the spiritual wickedness that we confront and understand how to leap over every wall and run through every troop of opposition. It is upon this battlefront that we come to understand how to be strong in the strength of the Lord and the power of His might.

We cannot weary in well doing, but instead remain bold and confident that what God says in His word is true. We must be willing to let God teach us to look past our senses and all the natural realm and rise up in the authority of Jesus. Satan is determined to achieve his goals and we must engage his armies with all the authority that has been given to us. Satan is full of pride and rebellion, and has come out to defy the armies of God. Just as he screamed back at Jesus and said, "I demand you by the Most High God leave us alone," he will scream at us as well. In his rebellion and pride he refuses to obey God and therefore must be forced by the power that is greater than his own. He will use every trick possible to convince us that he does not have to listen, but if we will not back down, the anointing will destroy his yoke. His craft and power are great and his tactics very subtle, but we have been given authority to crush him under foot. We have been given all power and authority to liberate all mankind from the treachery, torments and slavery that he works. God has given His saints all power over every unclean spirit to cast them out and to stop their works. We pray that this generation will fully discover the fullness of the ministry of Jesus and do the same works that He did and even greater works.

The Authority of the Kingdom of God

"This gospel of the kingdom must be preached in all the world for a witness unto all nations, and then the end shall come."

<u>Matthew 24:14</u>

The Kingdom of God is forever and ever. There is no greater realm, nor higher authority. It is the expression of the absolute and sovereign reign and authority of the Everlasting God. Although the prophet Enoch prophesied of it and Abraham sought for it, the power of the kingdom first began to be expressed through the nation of Israel under the leadership of Moses. When God separated a people to live under His dominion and rule, He stepped into the earthly realm of man – and the kingdom of God was revealed. He entrusted those whom He called out with kingdom authority, and displayed His sovereign power by overthrowing the greatest empires on the Earth. When God began to reveal that He ruled in the kingdoms of men, He did so with mighty signs and wonders. The power of His kingdom was wielded through the shepherd's staff of a seemingly defeated and ruined man named Moses. When the kingdom of God stepped in, His heavenly power over the elements and over the course of nature was demonstrated. The proof was provided that nothing existed outside the absolute dominion of God and His representatives; those to whom He had entrusted His authority. By this authority the Red Sea was rolled back, the Jordan River stacked up into the heavens, and Joshua, who was once a mere slave, commanded the sun and the moon to stand still. It was proven by His mighty acts that kings and nations, nature and its elements, even life and death were subject to the sovereign commands of the Almighty God.

All of these things were only preparation for the greatest event of all: in the fullness of time, Jesus Christ came to reveal the fullness of the kingdom. The King of the kingdom came when the time had finally come to declare ultimate war on the kingdom of darkness and to liberate men. The kingdom of God stepped into the world through Jesus Christ the King. Though He came humbled as a servant, the mandate of His ministry was to declare the kingdom of God and demonstrate the authority of the kingdom. Jesus went everywhere preaching the kingdom of God, and casting out everything that belonged to the realm of darkness. All-out war had begun against every demon spirit who had taken over the lives of men. The King of the kingdom came proclaiming deliverance and salvation to all those who had been held in the spiritual prison of death. Every demon had to relinquish its hold on those whom they had controlled and tormented. The authority of the kingdom of God was invading the lives of men, and no darkness could resist. Jesus was the true light that was shining, for a new day had dawned. The devils had no choice but to go, and every prisoner who would believe was set free. The declaration by the Captain of our salvation that the Kingdom of God had come was sounded out definitively when Jesus said, "If I work miracles and cast out devils by the Spirit of God, then the kingdom of God has come to you[1]." The mission of Jesus Christ the Messiah was to destroy the works of the devil; and everywhere His gospel is preached unto this day, Satan has to go! Under the dominion of the ministry of Jesus, all demon spirits lose their claims on all who would seek refuge in the kingdom of God and of His Christ.

The Works of the Kingdom

Everyone has to agree that when Jesus preached the gospel of the kingdom it was with mighty signs and wonders. His style of preaching was to cast out every devil that He encountered and to heal all manner of sickness and disease.[2] When the light of life began to shine, the kingdom of darkness could not remain! Jesus demonstrated that when the kingdom of God was present, there would be a display of the power of God. It was impossible for the liberator of men to come and do anything less than deliver men from the power of sin and death. His works were the proofs that He was sent from the Father and came in the power of the kingdom.[3] Whenever the ministry of Jesus was encountered, those same works were always present.

When John the Baptist had a moment of uncertainty of who Jesus was, it would be the works of Jesus' ministry that would settle all questions. When John's disciples came to Jesus, they watched as those who had plagues and diseases were cured and those possessed by devils were set free. He told the disciples to go and tell John, "the blind see, the lame walk, the lepers are cleansed, the deaf hear, the dead are raised, to the poor the gospel is preached."[4] This was the poof of Jesus' ministry then. It was the proof of Jesus' ministry in the book of Acts and it is the proof of Jesus' ministry today – it is the gospel of the kingdom!

The Kingdom Revealed

The first request that Jesus had of those who would be a part of His kingdom was to come and follow Him.[5] Jesus would teach them and train them to function in the authority of His ministry. The first things Jesus trained His disciples in was how to destroy the works of the devil[6] wherever they encountered Satan afflicting and tormenting men. As the representatives of the kingdom of God, they were given authority over every demon spirit to cast them out. As the fighting men of David were invincible against the Philistines, even more invincible were those who had been entrusted with the authority of the Kingdom under the ministry of Jesus. The reign of Christ was only beginning, and those who had joined in to follow Him were made invincible against all their foes; and, nothing within the realms of darkness could harm them.[7] It was their assignment to do the same works of Jesus, and declare through their works that the Kingdom of God had come.[8] Never had such power been given to men. Jesus had come to cast out Satan and to destroy His dominion,[9] the demonstration of His absolute power and authority over all of the works of darkness had begun, and the means by which it took shape was through the preaching of the gospel.

Hindus in Nepal, coming the Jesus Christ by the multitudes

The mission that was assigned to the disciples of Jesus was exactly the same as that of their Lord. They were given the assignment to go and cast out devils, heal the sick, and raise the dead. They were to go everywhere and render the power of

Satan ineffectual, and restore and make whole those things that the powers of darkness had ruined. They were to do all of this in the authority of the kingdom of God. The proclamation of the gospel was the announcement that the kingdom of God had come – through the demonstration of the Spirit and power. The gospel both announces and proves the undeniable and absolute authority of God over all things. It is the declaration that Satan will no longer be allowed to execute His will unchallenged by the armies of God! Therefore, we are given the authority to bind on Earth any power of darkness that we encounter. In the authority of the kingdom we are able to loose every prisoner and open every prison door, proclaiming liberty to all mankind everywhere.[10] The message of the kingdom is this: the days of your captivity are over! As we bind on Earth, God in cooperation with us will bind in Heaven; and whatever we would set free on Earth, God will set free in Heaven – so that the ministry of Jesus through us will look the same today as it did then.

Pastor Mark ministering by the Spirit

The authority of the kingdom was not limited to the 12 apostles or to the 70 other disciples, but given for the entirety of the church age – to whoever would believe.[11] The church was not a first century phenomenon, but the very expression of the power of the kingdom of God on Earth. So long as Christ Jesus reigns, the kingdom of God will be shown to be the supreme power; and of His kingdom there shall be no end. The supreme authority of Christ was forever finalized when He through His death, burial, and resurrection destroyed the power of the devil. Satan and all his host were stripped of all their authority and were shown to be absolutely defeated by Jesus.[12] That authority and supremacy of Christ was transferred to the church, which upholds and enforces all of His vested interest. The authority of the church, which Jesus purchased with His own blood and baptized in the Holy Spirit, will remain effective and powerful; and not even the gates of hell can prevail against it. The church is unstoppable and undefeatable, for it is the fullness of God on the Earth, and its head is the King of Kings. The church finds itself collectively and individually seated together in the highest place of authority with Christ Jesus: at the right hand of the Father.[13] We have been given the absolute authority to execute His judgments in the Earth.

The Power of His Might

All of the power by which God created all things, the might by which He in His sovereign power threw down everything opposed to Him, and the strength that He has possessed within Himself for all eternity has been given to the saints to be effective in this war.[14] Through this vested authority, we throw down and stop all spiritual wickedness, and all mights and powers that oppose the will of the King of kings and Lord of lords. The Holy Spirit desires to open our eyes, so that we can

The gospel of the kingdom must be preached over all the earth: Pastor Mark in Nepal with his interpreter Baal Shiva, ministering with the pastors and leaders of the Nepali churches. Background: Pastor Anne Spitsbergen and Evangelist John Ward

understand the exceeding greatness of God's power that was given to us when He raised Christ Jesus from the dead and set Him at His own right hand, far above all principalities and powers.[15] Paul, expressing the authority of the Kingdom given to him, said that he was commissioned to turn people from darkness to light and from the power of Satan unto God.[16] We must be equally focused on what we are called to do, and certain that we have been given the same authority to preach the gospel of the Kingdom.

The kingdom of God, which was first entrusted to Israel, is now witnessed through the church.[17] It is in the midst of the church that the fullness of God dwells and the manifestation of the glory of God is revealed. The church is inseparable from

Christ. It is the body or being of Christ, the head over all authorities and powers.[18] It is from the church that the prophets now come; that the apostles, teachers, miracles, and gifts of healing flow out. Even as Israel once had the supreme honor of representing God in the Earth and having His presence dwelling among them – that same honor and glory has been poured out upon the church. The church is the company of the kingdom of God, the citizens of Heaven made up of both Jews and Gentiles, for now all covenants and promises are fulfilled only in Christ Jesus.

The Revelation of the Kingdom

God showed Abraham the glory of the heavenly and allowed him to see the framework of the kingdom. His grandson Jacob received the revelation of just how close the kingdom of God was when he discovered that he was in the house of God and knew it not. Elisha's servant's eyes were opened so that he could understand that the sphere of the Earth was filled with the heavenly host. Nebuchadnezzar thought that his authority was superior to all others, but when brought to his senses he realized that God ruled in the kingdom of men. When Jesus stepped into the world, He rent the veil of the heavenly and everyone was allowed to witness a greater dimension of this truth – beholding the glory of the Father through the Only Begotten Son. The mystery of the kingdom came embodied in the person of the Lord Jesus Christ who came to invite all men everywhere to enter into this realm of God's eternal life. His power and dominion is an everlasting power and dominion, and His rule and reign is forever and ever.

Above all other things the saints must seek the kingdom of God. We must earnestly desire the kingdom of God to be revealed in our lives, in our ministries and to the world around us. As much as we are to seek the kingdom of God, we are to receive it. We not only pursue it, but find its life and goodness in Christ Jesus, for the abundant life is the life of the kingdom. Although the kingdoms of this world have not yet become the Kingdom of our Lord and of His Christ, all who have believed have been translated into the kingdom of the Son and are entrusted with the authority to demonstrate it.[19] As much as God was King over Israel, He is King over the church today. We must realize that the gospel of the Lord Jesus Christ is the gospel of the kingdom, which comes with the demonstration that God is in our midst and that Jesus is ruler over all things.[20] It was for this cause that we were endued with power to be His witnesses. The gospel of the kingdom must be preached in all the Earth and then the end will come. To think that the kingdom of God is less powerful and authoritative than it was in the days of Old or in the times and ministry of Jesus is a serious error, for now all the fullness of Jesus' ministry has come, with these works and greater!

The day of the Lord is about to explode upon the landscape of time. The kingdoms of this world shall soon become the Kingdom of our Lord and of His Christ. Today we are to lift up our voices and cry out to all men to flee from the wrath that is to come. We have been given the ability to stop the lies of Satan and the ability to deliver men from his power. Do not delay, for the day of the Lord is coming: "the Lord is coming forth out of His place, and will come down and tread upon the high places of the Earth. And the mountains will melt under Him, and the valleys will be cleft, like wax before the fire, like waters poured down a steep place" (Micah 1:3-4). "Prepare to meet your God..." (Amos 4:12)

The Gospel of the Kingdom

There is a risk that many who have been given access into the realms of the kingdom of God will fail to enter into it. Satan sets a trap of religion and ritual to snare all those who would desire to come into the kingdom. Israel fell into this trap and made their traditions more valuable than the will of God and through their traditions and ritual made void the Word of God. The same problem exists today. Many come in the name of the Lord ardently insisting that they are speaking the Word of God faithfully, yet they are constantly making void the Word of God by their traditions. They falsely proclaim, without any scriptural proof, that much of what the Bible says is not for today, but only belonged to the first century church. They think that they can replace the demonstration of the Spirit and power with liturgy and programs. They fail to realize that there must be a witness of the Holy Spirit in their lives now and without that witness they have no proof. As the champions of their denominations and dogmas, they forsake the very principles of the gospel of the kingdom.

Are we really to believe that the gospel of the kingdom died with the apostle Paul? That Paul was the last one entrusted with the demonstration of the Spirit and power? To believe this, one will inevitably have to alter almost every word of the New Testament. Every dimension of the power and authority expressed by the activity of the Holy Ghost, from prophecy to the gifts of the Spirit, would have to be removed. The gospel would no longer truly be about what God the Holy Spirit does through the church to represent the will and kingdom of God, but rather what man can do. In this case the witness would no longer be heavenly but earthly. It would not be the Son speaking from Heaven but an earthly voice of humanity now heard. If we remove the element of signs and wonders then we have to remove Jesus the miracle worker from the midst of the church. How could we expect to believe that Jesus is present in our assemblies if He is to be a different Jesus now? He would no longer be the Jesus who heals the sick and delivers men from the oppression of the devil. He would be a silent Jesus who is there to hear us sing and pray. If we remove the element of divine power from the prayers that we pray how is it anything more than vain repetition? Petitions brought before God that require His intervention and His own working power can be classed as nothing less than signs and wonders. I assure you that the gospel of the kingdom is being preached today and anything else is another gospel.

The Authority of the Spirit of God

The Holy Spirit has come. His glory and grace has been poured out upon all flesh. He has come to take the place of Jesus as the supreme authority on the Earth. Although Jesus is head of the Church, it is the Holy Spirit who executes all of His will.[21] He was sent by the Father to be our teacher, mentor, and our guide. Although the early apostles and disciples had the Lord Jesus to show them how to walk in the power and authority of the Kingdom they still needed the accompanying presence and revelation that only the Holy Spirit could bring. Until the Holy Spirit came they could not fully understand nor function in all that the Father had planned for them to have. The Holy Spirit has come to show us how to do the works of Christ and represent the kingdom. He has come to reveal Jesus to us and to also reveal Him in our lives. Everything He does is about glorifying the risen Christ.

It is an awesome thing to consider that God would want to display His mighty power and authority through us, but it is even more wonderful to know that He has come to live and dwell in our lives.[22] All we need to do is learn to be obedient to the leadership of the Holy Spirit and all the glory of Christ Jesus will be realized. God is dedicated to training us in all the ways of His majesty and power. It is His will that His glory be expressed through our words and deeds. The beauty and splendor of God's life will be revealed in us as we walk in the ways of the Holy Ghost.

The Holy Spirit was given to us as a sacred gift from the Father and the Lord Jesus Christ.[23] God ordained that we should have the same baptism that Jesus was baptized with – that same divine power and authority. In His love and affection for us, He poured out His best: the gift of the Holy Ghost. Through the Holy Spirit we have been given the glory of the Father and of Jesus Christ. Now by the Holy Spirit the glory and majesty of His way flow through us like rivers. Our lives have become like the garden of God where every good thing grows. In this fellowship divine with the Father, the Son and the Holy Spirit, God would show us how to be overwhelmed with His goodness by taking in the currents of His life.

The special anointing that Jesus received was the unlimited supply of the power of the Holy Spirit. When Jesus ascended up on High, the same works that He did and even greater works as well were promised to all who would believe. There was no one in the history of man that had the mantle of the Holy Ghost like Jesus. He was given the unlimited ability to reveal the glory and majesty of the Father.[24] Jesus, who was compelled to be like us in all things, also gave us everything He had. He gave us that same glory, that same mantle, so that we may be shown to be in Him. Our heavenly calling and divine purpose is to walk even as He walked and demonstrate the power and authority of His resurrection.[25] For this purpose, Jesus baptized us in the Holy Ghost and power.[26]

Jesus did not step out and begin to demonstrate the will of the Father and reveal the kingdom of God until He was baptized in the Holy Spirit. How much less can we? And, if we are to have His ministry, then we must have His baptism! The Holy Ghost is the first-fruits of our salvation and God's divine life restored to man; He is also the One who empowers us to bear witness of Jesus and gives us everything that belongs to Him. Those who had been with Jesus, who were developed under His ministry and sent out with His divine power, had to wait until they received power from on High before they could preach. How could we possibly think that things would be any different for us today? If anything, we are in greater need of the same outpouring from on High. If the apostles could not be His witnesses without this baptism, how much less can we?

The same encounter with the Holy Spirit is for every generation! The outpouring of the Holy Spirit is not just for the day of Pentecost and for the apostles but for every house like that of Cornelius, for the Holy Spirit has been poured out upon all flesh.[27] The anointing of Jesus and the baptism in the Holy Spirit is for as many as the Lord our God shall call. The Holy Spirit has not left us, He is here on the Earth right now. To forsake the working and the manifestation of His power is to forsake the ministry of Christ. All we must do is recognize that this is God's command, and then begin to cooperate with His will. We simply cannot be proof-providers of who Jesus is until we receive this power from on High. Let your faith soar by believing that this is the Father's will and receive the Holy Ghost right now!

Jesus the Baptizer

One of the first things revealed about Jesus was that He would be the great baptizer who would baptize those who would believe in the Holy Ghost.[28] Jesus being the first one baptized in the Spirit without measure would be the One that would release God's gift upon the redeemed.[29] Jesus ushered in the age of the Kingdom and was anointed to throw down all opposing forces. The King of Kings and Lord of Lords also empowered us to bring an end to Satan's works. The one who torments men with sin, sickness and disease would be destroyed through the operation of the Holy Ghost. The mantle of the Spirit of the Lord was poured out upon His church to overthrow the powers of darkness that exist in every generation. It is only by the Holy Ghost that the works of the devil can be stopped. The baptism in the Spirit fills us and surrounds us with the kingdom authority of Jesus. Without the Holy Spirit, Jesus will not be seen and we will be powerless to do anything.

Before Jesus, men only received the Spirit by measure. The measure of the Spirit that they received supplied them with a limited ability to do the work of God. By the Spirit, Elijah was caught away, did miracles, called fire down out of Heaven and heard the plans of the foreign kings which they had spoken in their secret chambers. Elijah received an anointing by the Holy Ghost and the measure that he received was doubled for His servant Elisha. Their works were mighty and glorious but they were still limited by the measure of the Spirit that they were given. The portion of the Spirit allowed Elijah to raise one man from the dead. The double portion given to Elisha empowered him to raise two men from the dead.

It was by way of a special yet limited anointing that the prophets of old prophesied and delivered to us the Word of God. By a measure of the Holy Spirit, Moses spoke to a rock and water came out and the stone of flint became a pool of water. Moses imparted a measure of the portion that He received to Joshua his servant. Then by the Spirit of the Lord Joshua commanded the Sun and Moon to stand still. By the anointing of the Holy Ghost, Samson and the judges worked their mighty works. By the Spirit of the Lord, David threw down the enemies of Israel, sung his songs and was found to have a heart like God. Today the anointing that we have received is not by measure but the unlimited one of Jesus. Christ Jesus is our Master and as His servants we must obey. It is in His ministry that we walk and not one of our own. Our dedication to Him should be far greater than Elisha's dedication to serve his master Elijah. Should we not rejoice in the call and with complete abandonment give up everything to follow Him?

Many have come up with different ideas about the baptism of the Holy Spirit and what it should produce. One thing should be obvious to everyone: it produced the ministry of Jesus in those who received it.[30] To believe that the same baptism would result in anything different than the ministry of Jesus is out of line with what Jesus said.[31] We must not represent a different Jesus than that same Jesus who turned the water into wine, raised the dead to life again and walked upon the stormy sea. It is His authority that we have received, who by the Spirit commanded the unclean spirits and they obeyed. This is the gospel that must be preached: the gospel of Jesus that proclaims liberty.

It was by this special baptism of the Holy Spirit and authority that John identified Jesus and gave witness that He was indeed the Christ. All of John's concerns were satisfied by the unlimited display of power in the ministry of Jesus. There was no need to look for another, because the crippled walked and the blind were made to see. The unlimited authority of the Holy Ghost that was poured out to set every person free was demonstrated by Jesus who went about doing good and healing all that were oppressed by the devil. This is the ministry of Jesus: the baptism in the Holy Ghost. The last days anointing of Jesus is the power from on High to cast out devils and preach the gospel to the poor. This is the gospel of the kingdom that must be preached and with bold authority we must say, "The Spirit of the Lord is upon Me, because He has anointed Me to preach the gospel to the poor; He hath sent Me to heal the brokenhearted, to preach deliverance to the captives, and recovering of sight to the blind, to set at liberty them that are bruised, to preach the acceptable year of the Lord (Luke 4:18-19)."

Co-inheritors In an Unlimited Gift

"The One that God sent speaks the words of God for God gives Him the Spirit without limits. The Father loves the Son and has placed all things in His hand. The one that believes in the Son has ageless (immeasurable) life"

John 3:34-36

Although Jesus was the Word and the eternal God, He laid aside all of His glory and became the Son of Man.[32] Jesus was God made flesh who became a man to reveal the Living Word. He not only came to pay for our sins at Calvary, but also to show us how to live our lives in the flesh. He was the pattern Son who condemned sin in the flesh and has given us an understanding so that we may know how to please the Father. It is His life that we have now inherited through this so great a salvation. We are not to live our own lives or have our own ministries, but rather that of Christ Jesus! God was incarnated into flesh the day that Christ was born, but His ministry did not begin until He received power from on High. Jesus' ministry began that day when He was baptized in the Holy Spirit and the voice came from Heaven.[33] At that time He was given the special anointing to preach the gospel of the kingdom. By the outpouring of the Holy Spirit upon His life He was given the fullness of divine power to preach and reveal the Father's will.[34]

The most remarkable thing is that God in His love has given to us this unspeakable gift that we should be co-inheritors with Jesus.[35] We have been given all His fullness and made complete in Him.[36] Every person who will believe has been given the opportunity to live in the fullness of Christ Jesus: in relationship with the Father, baptism in the Holy Ghost and the authority to preach the gospel. In our fellowship with Him we can comprehend with all the saints every dimension of the love of Christ and be filled with all the fullness of God.[37] God not only gave us this amazing opportunity – He demands it of our lives. We are called to follow Jesus; yes, even to live His life! We must not draw back but receive this call to walk in oneness with Him in His anointing.

Hindus receiving the word of the Lord Jesus Christ

Each one of us really has only one of two choices: we will either accept the call to the fullness of Christ and mature by the Spirit into the full measure of His ministry or we will remain as defeated and incapable infants (nepios) that have no stability.[38] If we will believe what Christ Jesus said and believe what He has given, then we will receive the ability to move in His unlimited authority and power and oneness with God. Through the Holy Ghost the flood gates of Heaven are released within our souls to flow out into a dry and thirsty land as rivers of life. These living waters are the expression of God's own immeasurable and unlimited life. We may confidently say that through Christ Jesus we have received an immeasurable and abundant life by an unlimited supply of the Spirit.

God dwells in us

All these things that God has done for our lives are too wonderful for us! The good news is that we do not have to rely upon ourselves to accomplish all of these great things in God for it is Christ in us that will do the work! God walks in us, lives in us, speaks through us and acts through our lives. We can say that He sees through our eyes and hears through our ears. We may be insensitive to the living presence of God in us, but if we are willing to yield ourselves completely over to the instruction of the Holy Spirit we will become aware of all that God would do in and through our members.[39] We have been given the mind of Christ and the Spirit of the Son.[40] The foundation of the faith is that Christ dwells in us. He is the greater One that is in us. He is the One who has come with the Father and they've made their dwelling in us.[41] It is Jesus who dwells in us by the Holy Spirit, who He has given us. He is both with us and in us and we are to walk in Him, live in Him and conduct ourselves by His desires. We are joined to the Lord and are One Spirit with Him.[42] We are called the temple of the Holy Ghost. We have received the same glory that Father gave to Jesus and are made one with Him just as He is One with the Father: Jesus in us and the Father in Jesus so that we can be perfect in this oneness.[43]

One of the absolutes of the New Covenant is that we are to be those that represent God and stand in the place of Jesus. So in order to fully represent Jesus, we have been given the power and authority that we need; Christ in us our confidence of glory. It was by the Holy Ghost that Jesus was incarnated into the womb of Mary and it is by the same Spirit of the Lord that we have been born again. Jesus was baptized in the Holy Spirit to preach the gospel of the kingdom and so we too have been baptized with the same Spirit to preach this gospel of the dear Son. We are both commissioned and empowered to represent the kingdom. We are not of this world and are just like Him because we have been translated into His kingdom and baptized in His power.[44]

Strengthened by the Spirit

If we are going to walk in the authority of the Spirit, then we must learn to be strengthened by the Spirit. Paul's instructions to the church were to be continually filled with the Spirit in order to be the witnesses that they should be.[45] They were to have the life of Christ, His righteousness, peace and joy by the Holy Ghost.[46] They were to abound in faith and expectation by the power of the Holy Spirit. To have these things we must learn

Pastor Mark ministering by the Spirit

how to put up the sails and yield to Him. As the wind, He will take us where we are to go. He will teach us to master even the smallest whisper of His inspirations that takes us where He leads. There can be no oar or rudder on this river for God must be fully in control – all we need to do is relax and yield and He will take us where we are to go. He will show us and fill us with everything that belongs to Jesus and the Father as we learn to walk with Him.

Bringing the needy to Jesus

Fundamental to the New Covenant is the outpouring of the Holy Ghost upon the church. Through this baptism in the Holy Spirit, God will strengthen you and empower you with a continual infilling. He will make you strong simply by cooperating with Him as the Word of God describes. You will discover that through praise and thanksgiving it is easy to enter into that place of being completely yielded. As you begin to sing and make melody in your heart, the Holy Spirit will fill you up and as you're filled the flow just continues to get stronger. As you pray in the Holy Ghost, He will build you up and establish you in this communion.[47] When you are in need of love, joy and peace, He supplies it freely when you ask and depend on Him for what you need. Walking in the Spirit and living by the

Spirit is a life committed to relying on the Holy Spirit and not yourself. God sees those who turn to Him and depend on Him and He rewards us with His presence and His abundant life. The supply of all these good things is like a river flowing from our hearts and there are no limits or restrictions on the one that will yield to Him. The hookup with the Spirit was made at Pentecost. It was there that we observe what happened when the Teacher came to lead and to guide. A divine connection was made when the Spirit began to speak through those who simply obeyed and waited for God to fill them.

To this end we are strengthened that we might live and move by Him. Just like Paul, we will preach by the power of the Holy Ghost with the demonstration of the Holy Spirit and power. His testimony was that he had fully preached the gospel with mighty signs and wonders and by the power of the Spirit of God.[48] If we take the working of the Holy Ghost out of the gospel that Paul preached we are left with no living relationship with Jesus. There would be no power to advance the gospel and bring people to salvation. There would be no authority of the church to function in. Without the Holy Spirit that Paul gave witness to, there would have to be a new design and pattern for the way that the church is to operate. Instead of the manifestation of the Spirit given to every man, there would be only the manifestation of men. The words of knowledge, miracles, and gifts of healing would no longer exist. The Apostles, Prophets, Evangelists, Pastors and Teachers would not be able to function without this special anointing. There would be no more prophecy. There would be no more utterances of the Spirit; Heaven would be silent. The rivers of God would no longer flow from our bellies and we would live in a dry and thirsty land where there is no water.

"Then I remembered the words of the Lord when He said, 'John truly baptized with water but you shall be baptized in the Holy Ghost.'"

Acts 11:16

The witness of the Holy Spirit in the salvation of the Gentiles was paramount. Without the outpouring of the Holy Ghost and the evidence of speaking in the heavenly language, there would have been no way for there to be the certainty that the Gentiles were also granted the same gift of salvation that had been given to Israel. When the Holy Ghost was poured out, everyone who received on the day of Pentecost spoke with these heavenly tongues of fire. John the Baptist gave witness to the Holy Ghost and fire that Jesus would baptize in. These are the rivers: God's special gift. Man's opinion should be of little value. The baptismal ministry of Jesus looks like Pentecost with tongues of fire and prophecy.[49]

The ministry of Jesus and the gift of the Holy Spirit are inseparable. Jesus began His ministry through the outpouring of the Holy Spirit upon His life, and He started His church by pouring out the Holy Spirit upon it. As much as Jesus is the Savior, He is also the Baptizer. His ministry as Baptizer did not begin until He ascended to the throne of God. Jesus told all of Jerusalem that the gift of God was available, but it was noted that the gift would not come upon them until after He was seated at the right hand of the Father and glorified.[50] Just before He was about to leave for the final time after His resurrection, Jesus reminded His disciples of what John had said about His ministry.[51] When Peter referred to the Gentiles receiving the Holy Ghost, it was in the context of that same baptismal ministry which they received on Pentecost – proving that the gift of God was available to all.[52] Paul also made the same connection to the baptismal ministry of Jesus in his address to the disciples at Ephesus; and by-and-large left them without choice in the matter.[53]

There are two primary gifts highlighted in the New Testament: the gift of salvation and the gift of the Holy Spirit.[54] The New Testament does not make an argument for them being divided between two different classes of Christians. Why would anyone, after giving their life to Jesus and receiving the transforming work of grace, refuse to receive the baptismal ministry of the One who saved them? How can anyone believe that the ministry of Jesus is different today than it was yesterday, or that the working of the Holy Spirit has changed? To dispute that the baptismal ministry of Jesus is accompanied by anything other than the gift of tongues, one must argue from the traditions and philosophy of men –the scripture establishes its certainty. Paul, who was the chief defender of the gift and the one who spoke in tongues more than them all, did not in any way detract from this truth. Paul's rhetorical question on the gift of tongues in 1 Corinthians 12:30 may be applied in several ways, and clearly does not disqualify any or all believers from functioning in this gift. Besides, no one can make a doctrine out of one single verse of scripture, especially when its supposed application would be in direct contradiction to other witnesses.

The witness of the Holy Spirit in our life should be more important to us than the witness of men. The confirmation that God brings should be more important than the confirmation of a denomination. The baptism in the Holy Spirit should be more precious and sought after than the baptism in water. The house of Cornelius had this witness, confirmation, and baptism; which were the proofs that Peter used to convince the church at

Jerusalem that God had also extended all grace to the Gentiles as well as to the Jews. Peter so integrates the baptism in the Holy Spirit with redemption that He applied it to the prophesy of Joel, with regards to what would be poured out upon all flesh – making the baptism in the Spirit and its prophetic witness something that belongs to everyone. Peter made the baptismal ministry of Jesus available to everyone when He coupled it with the call to salvation, saying: "Repent everyone of you, and be baptized in the name of Jesus Christ for the remission of sins, and you shall receive the gift of the Holy Ghost" (Acts 2:38).

Greater Works

"These works which I do shall you also do and greater works than these because I go to my Father"
John 14:12

There is a divine hookup with God through the Holy Ghost, an authority to do these works that Jesus did and greater works as well. One may argue that the disciples had an advantage over us: they had Jesus to model Heaven before them every day and to show them how to walk in this unlimited authority. It was faith-building being around Jesus, watching as He ministered the things of the Spirit and did the works of the Father. Yet Jesus told His disciples that He had something better for them. He was going to send them the Holy Spirit so that they could learn the things of Heaven more effectively.[55] Jesus would go to the Father and be exalted to the position of absolute authority and send the Holy Ghost. They would be baptized with the same Holy Ghost and fire that He had and would continue to do His works and even greater works. These works testify that Jesus did not die. They testify that He was raised up from the dead and given all authority in Heaven and in Earth. Should we believe that there is no reason for Jesus to be so glorified today?

Testifying to the miraculous!

If these works are to be done through our lives, then we must give ourselves to the things of the Spirit. We will grow and mature into every dimension of the ministry that Jesus described if we are willing to pay the same price, deny ourselves, take up our cross, and follow Him. All we need to do is begin to give the Holy Spirit the proper place of leadership and no longer walk after our own interest. We must be willing to learn how to submit our hearts and mouths to the things that He is saying. If we yield our emotions and our passions to His divine inspirations we will find that we have the most personal Teacher who will give us spiritual understanding. We can begin to live in Spirit knowledge rather than human reasoning. Our eyes can see what eyes have never seen before and our hearts understand what has never entered into the heart of man.[56] The influence of the Holy Spirit will have more impact on us than the influences of the world if we are willing to mind the things of the Spirit. If we will live our lives by the Holy Spirit, then the light of His glory will shine through us – the power and authority that witnesses that we are in Him and He is in us, and that it is Christ that does the works, not us. If we refuse to lay our hands on the sick, then how will we ever be strengthened in that faith? If we refuse to stand up boldly in the authority of the Spirit and command the devils to go, then how will we ever be strengthened in the authority that comes by doing what God commands?

These works that God ordained are the testimony of an intimate relationship with Him. The works that Jesus did were the works that the Father did through Him. They were the testimony of the oneness that He had with the Father. They proved that He was the Christ the Savior of the world. The works that Christ Jesus desires now to do through us are the testimony that He dwells in us and we dwell in Him. The proof is that He is the Redeemer who fully ransomed man, that we are not our own but bought with a price and now live our life by Him. These works of Jesus are the testimony that He is the exalted King of kings and reigns supremely over all. These works are the testimony of our oneness with Him, of the love that the Father has given us through Him that "whatever we ask" He will do that the Father may be glorified in the Son.[57] This kind of relationship that produces the works and ministry of Jesus is only possible by the power of the Holy Ghost. The testimony of Christ Jesus' unlimited authority is the authority of the Spirit revealed in us today. By the authority of the Spirit we testify that Christ Jesus is the Savior of the world who has conquered everything.

The Authority of the Word

The word reveals everything that we know about God. God has exalted His word above His name and it is forever settled in Heaven.[58] The Word of God may be understood as the supreme authority of both His will and His plan. It was by the authority of the word that all things were created.[59] It was also by the authority of the word that we have been redeemed. The "Word was made Flesh" that we might behold the Living Word Christ Jesus who revealed the fullness of all divine power. The Word of God is the life changing power of God that makes all things new.

The Word of God is the expression of all divine authority. It declares the sovereign will of God. There is no power in Heaven or hell or upon the Earth that can stop the authority of God's word. The Word of God is living, it is Spirit and life and it is by the Word of God that we live too. Just like the manna that came down from Heaven to feed the children of Israel, the true bread of life, Christ Jesus, has come that we may live by Him. We are taught of God that we live by every word that proceeds out of His mouth. This is the word that we are to preach by the Holy Ghost sent down from Heaven.[60] As we meditate upon the word and give ourselves to its study we are built up and established to do the works of Jesus.[61]

The word describes our life and what God has created us to be. It defines our expectations and describes reality. Our circumstances cannot be defined by our own perceptions, for only the Word of God is truth – everything else is a lie of deception. The Word of God is the absolute and final authority on every issue that we encounter. It is the means by which we look into the realms of the spiritual and understand what God is doing. It declares to us the truth that the Holy Spirit brings to life. It describes the actions that God takes by His Spirit in our hearts.

If we fail to believe the word, we will be deprived of the blessing that God has supplied. For the word to work mightily in us we must believe.[62] God's word must be mixed with faith! God has given us an absolute guarantee that His word is true. It is easier for Heaven and Earth to pass away than for any of His promises to fail.[63] If we speak God's word, not mixed with our opinion and ideas, then we will get God's results. "Well done" will be the words heard by everyone who is willing to not only hear, but also be obedient and do what God has spoken.[64] Let Jesus become the darling of your heart so that no matter how impossible the situation may be, all you need is to hear His word that bids you to come. The Word of God gives us the authority to supersede the laws of nature. The Word of God is powerful, expressing the faith that calls those things that are not as though they were and they come into existence![65] The Word of God is sharper than any two edged sword, revealing the thoughts and intents of the heart, exposing everything. It is in our hearts and in our mouths; just believe it and speak it.[66] The word is the truth; it is sanctifying and, like the washing of water, it cleanses. [67] It is the incorruptible seed that lives and abides forever. All else will pass away, but the word will remain; it is the final judgment now and in the future.

Speaking the Word

*"The centurion answered and said, 'Lord I am not worthy
that you should come under my roof but speak the word
only and my servant shall be healed'"*

Matthew 8:8

The centurion presented a case for authority and described how to place a value on someone's word. He described a word as only being as good as the authority of the person who gave it. When it comes to God's authority, we can be certain that there is none greater. The centurion understood authority because he had been vested by the Roman Empire with the position to command men. The centurion, being a man of authority and being subject to men with great authority, was able to recognize the authority that Jesus had. He may have heard Jesus speak the words of life that day on the mountain. He may have also heard Him tell the man with leprosy that he was healed and then watched the immediate transformation. Whatever the situation was in which this man had encountered Jesus, he recognized an authority that was greater than any authority that he had ever seen before. He recognized that Jesus had authority that extended beyond the ordinary and whatever He said would result in the miracle that he needed. For the centurion, all that Jesus had to do was "speak the word only."

When the apostles found their lives in peril, Peter rose up with confidence in Christ and only needed the word to be spoken: Jesus' command to come.[68] His life was threatened by a terrible storm, but he found certainty and confidence in Jesus. When He saw the Master of the wind and the waves, he was no longer in peril or gripped with the fear of death. Like the centurion, all that Peter needed was for Christ Jesus to speak the word and he would master what had threatened his life. Through the word, Peter was empowered to do what no man had ever done before and by the word of Christ he too stood with Jesus over all the earthly realm. Christ Jesus bids us to come and walk with Him, but His word alone must be enough. He has invited everyone who will hear to come and walk in the heavenly supernatural realm.

We Speak the Word of God

"Because of this also we give thanks to God continually that when you received the word you heard from us you received it not as the word of men but as it is in truth the Word of God which also works mightily in you that believe."

1 Thessalonians 2:13

Everything that we know about the will of God and the authority that He has given us is revealed through His word that was delivered to us as a Bible. If we fail to believe the Word of God, we are left powerless and faithless. God has given us the authority of His word to speak and then from that word of faith have signs, wonders and miracles. We cannot rehearse our doubts and fears and have the display of the power of God. If we speak His word and declare those things that God will do, then we will discover that God is in our midst bringing His word that we speak to life by His Holy Spirit.

Some people choose only to believe parts of the Word of God, but if we will believe everything that God has said in His word, all that He has promised will be ours! The seed of God's word has been planted in us and will bring forth its fruit if there is an obedient and yielded heart. So many people fail to yield;

instead they stand around all of their lives questioning instead of acting. When the Word of God came into our lives it produced the greatest miracle of all: a new heart and a new spirit that made us one with God.[69] That same Word of God spoken through our mouths will transform others too. Can there be any greater miracle than a transformed life? Can there be any greater faith than to believe that we will be raised from the dead to life eternal? Why then would we fail to believe all those other signs, wonders and gifts of faith and power?

If you will believe, then the same miracle-working power of God's word that was in the mouth of Jesus will be in your mouth too. You will speak those things which God has spoken and the miracle will take place. When you command what God commands, then demons will have to flee. When the Word of God is spoken with the authority that He has given, the crippled will walk, the blind will see and the dead will be raised to life again. It is God's word that is working mightily in you – just step out and start doing that which seems impossible. God's word is verifiable and we can safely risk everything by believing and doing what it says. It can never pass away – it is powerful and living, so speak it now! We may have to confront many things that would oppose the Word of God but if we stand and refuse to back down we will surely see it work in and through our lives.

The Word of God produces within us the works of God. The Word of God produces more than just those works that the natural man can do, but it produces the mighty works that only the power of God can bring to pass.[70] If we think as mere men, then we will never step beyond the boundaries and limits of a natural world and what we as men can do.[71] The Word of God will not be of profit to us for the healing of our bodies if we fail to agree with it and do not allow faith to work through it.[72] It will never be the word of authority in our mouth that commands demons to go and deliverance to come.[73] Mountains will not be moved, storms will not be calmed and the dead will not be raised to life again. The fruits of, "whatsoever we ask," will never be witnessed through our lives and the will of God will not be accomplished in us. Joshua spoke with the word of authority and the sun and moon stood still. Jesus spoke and the wind and the waves obeyed. Paul spoke and commanded the crippled to walk and they stood upright on their feet. We believe and speak, for Christ Jesus has given us His word of authority to do His works.[74]

God Confirms His Word

"And they went and preached everywhere, the Lord working with them establishing the word through the miracles that followed. Amen."

Mark 16:20

Preaching the gospel can only be accomplished by declaring the Word of God. The Word of God is proven to be indeed the Word of God by miracles. Jesus, the miracle worker, still goes everywhere with those whom he has sent, confirming His word with miracles. Jesus spoke the words of God and miracles were the proof that the Father gave.[75] The gospel is the word of deliverance: deliverance from sin, sickness and disease. When the word of life is preached by the gospel, the miracles of God will take place as people are saved, healed and set free. This is what we must expect if we are moving in God's faith. The Word of God is the announcement of God's will for men and if anyone hears that word and believes, they will receive the blessings it describes. The word must be preached with authority and not mere recitals like the scribes.[76]

Bringing the sick to Jesus!

The Lord Jesus is passionate about bringing all men to salvation. He is the one who upholds all things by the word of His power and He is the one that is present wherever the gospel is preached. He is present to work the miracles that the gospel declares if there is someone who will believe.[77] While it is true that many will not believe unless there are miracles, it must still be understood that the gospel is all about miracles taking place. [78] How can we believe that a person can receive salvation without a miracle? How will the strongholds of demonic power be broken unless there is the miracle-working power of Jesus present?[79] Surely when we preach we expect that men will be saved? Why should we believe that the miracle to save the soul is present yet the miracle to heal the body is absent? What proof has anyone that the gospel that Paul preached is any different today? Why are men so willing to believe another gospel, one that is absent of the working of Jesus and the power of the Holy Spirit? This is not the Word of God, and where the word is not believed there is no authority! Men make their experiences of greater importance than God's word. Just because they prayed or preached and did not get the results that the Word of God testifies of, they call it "passed away." We must believe the Word of God and count God faithful who has promised no matter what we see. We must be willing to stand firm in those things which God has spoken and press in for the maturity that is needed so that the works of Jesus might be fully realized. How can we believe that one single Word of God will fail us? How can we believe that we are following Jesus when we do not do His works? If we preach Jesus, then we must preach that He is the Savior, Healer, Deliverer and Baptizer– that He is the same yesterday, today and forever! If not, then we are preaching another gospel.

The Testimony of the Word

"So then they spent considerable time speaking boldly in the Lord who bore witness to His word of grace, granting signs and wonders to be done by their hands."

Acts 14:3

God, who upholds all things by the word of His power, gives witness to His word with signs and wonders.[80] The gospel is not the word of men, but it is the Word of God and the Lord is committed to proving it. Although these words of God come out of our mouth, they are not our words but God's. When we speak as the oracles of God, we speak with the same authority that Jesus used when He commanded the unclean spirits with His word and they came out.[81] It is not dependent upon us to perform the works that the word describes; we are just responsible to do it. It is Christ Jesus who dwells in us that does the works. We announce to men that they must be saved and those who believe are transformed by the Holy Ghost. We lay hands on the sick and it is the power of God that is present that causes them to recover. God has put this word of life in our mouth – all we must do is speak!

By the hands of God's ministers many signs and wonders were done so that faith could be established in the hearts of the people who heard the word. They preached the Word of God that said, "these signs shall follow them that believe" and so the signs were there to give witness to the word. They spoke the word, which Jesus said could not pass away and when they spoke, the miracles of the word took shape. They preached that where two or three were gathered in His name, He would be in their midst and Jesus was there to prove it. They told the people that Jesus had commanded them to do the same works that He had done and even greater works, so God confirmed the word because there was a faithful man to speak it.

God blessed us with unprecedented support and solidarity among the churches with over 200 churches and more than 2000 church leaders supporting the crusade.

Wherever the Word of God is preached, God watches over His word to perform it. We can be confident that what God has declared in His word He will also do. Those things that God did in the days of Paul, He will also do today because the gospel has not changed. Paul fully preached the gospel in the city of Iconium, declaring the whole counsel of God with mighty signs and wonders and He will do the same in whatever city you preach in as well. When the word goes forth, all the hearer must do is allow it to be mixed with faith and then the power that created the heavens and the Earth will be released upon their life. Let the word of life give you insight and revelation and see what God will do through you as you proclaim His word.

The Authority of the Name of Jesus

"And Jesus came speaking to them saying, 'All authority is given to me in Heaven and in Earth.'"

Matthew 28:18

The authority that Jesus displayed in His earthly ministry was like none that had ever been seen before. He cast out devils with His word, and commanded the stormy winds and waves and they obeyed. There was no sickness or disease that could defy His authority. He was God manifested in the flesh, baptized in the Holy Ghost and nothing was impossible for Him. Yet when He stepped into His resurrected glory, an even greater authority began. All authority in Heaven and Earth was given to Him when God raised Him up from the dead and set Him at His own right hand.

Jesus took hold of His authority and poured it out upon His church. The Holy Spirit, who is the Spirit of grace and power, came to testify that all authority in Heaven and Earth was placed in Jesus. The unlimited and absolute authority of Jesus was given to all who would believe and it was released through His name. God will open up the eyes of those who will believe and show them the exceeding greatness of His power that has been given through the One that He has raised up from the dead.[82] In His name and through faith in His name, every power in Heaven and Earth must obey. Every form of death and pain must flee away when the authority of Jesus' name is believed upon and applied.

It is by the name of Jesus that the miracle of salvation is given unto men.[83] When a person calls on the name of Jesus they are delivered from every evil thing, brought into the family of God and given the blessings and protection of His household. God created Adam in His image and likeness and by the name of Jesus, a new spirit and a new heart is created in those who will believe.[84] The person who once was dominated by the power of Satan is given the divine nature by the washing of regeneration.[85] By the name of Jesus everything must change – for nothing can resist His power.[86] All powers and authorities, whether in nature, in the realm of men, in the realm of demon spirits, in Heaven, or in Earth are subject to His name and must obey what Jesus says. When we speak in His name, it is the same as Jesus speaking.

Whatever We Ask in the Name of Jesus

Our heavenly Father has made a pledge through His Son, that whatever we ask in the name of Jesus, He will do. The Father will grant the petition and show His outstretched hand because He is devoted to glorifying Jesus. He glorified the name of Jesus during the time of His ministry as a man and He is all the more devoted to glorifying the name of Jesus now. We are to ask and when we realize the relationship we have been given with the Father, our joy will be full. The display of God's grace upon us will be witnessed in our lives, for this is the fruit that God ordained for us to bear. The fruit of our lives must be asking for what we will and having our request granted by the Father.[87] In that day, when Jesus rose and ascended and the Holy Spirit was given, a new kind of authority was displayed in the life of all God's servants. The event would be so radical and so life changing that we would know that Christ is in us and that the Father is in Him. The name that the Father gave Jesus would be glorified by the greatest display of power the world had ever seen in men. It would be shown that as the Father was with Jesus even so He would be with us. It was by the Father that Jesus did His works and it would be by the Father and Christ Jesus that we would do these works and greater works than these. The name that is above all other names would be glorified as those redeemed by the blood of the Lamb would ask and the Father in Heaven would answer.

The Father has highly exalted the name of Jesus and at His name every knee must bow. The reign of Jesus has begun. He was crowned 2000 years ago when He ascended up on High. He is seated on His throne at the right hand of the Father until all His enemies are made His footstool. Of the increase of His government there will never be an end. The authority of His name will never lose its power! Jesus was glorified with the glory that He had with the Father before the world began. And when we speak that name, all Heaven is mobilized to answer our request – for there is no higher power.

God the Father is devoted to showing the world that we are His people that are ransomed by His Son. He wants to glorify the name of Jesus through our lives in view of everyone. The kind of relationship that has been given to us is that of a Father and a son. The riches of the inheritance are in us because Jesus brought us into the family. There is a proof that Jesus is the first begotten of many brethren and that is the witness of His ministry and His relationship with the Father in us. It is Father's good pleasure to give us the kingdom now that we are His heirs and co-inheritors with His Son. He wants us to ask in the name of Jesus so that this relationship may shine as a light unto the world. This is a relationship of love where we take pleasure in obeying His commands and He takes pleasure in doing whatever we ask. Through this relationship, we know that Jesus is in the Father and we are in Christ Jesus.[88] It is from this kind of relationship that the greater works are done.

Miracles in the Name of Jesus

"In the name of Jesus" is the most powerful utterance that can be heard through the mouths of the saints. Through His name, authority and power to do miracles has been given. Jesus said, "These miracles (signs) shall follow those who believe: in My name they shall cast out devils, they will speak with new tongues. Should they take up a snake or drink something deadly, they shall not be hurt. They shall lay hands on the sick and they shall recover." (Mark 16:17-18). The authority and faith that comes by the name of Jesus gives us the power to speak, and devils must obey. The power to cast out devils was always first in the list when Jesus described the authority that He had given to His servants. The authority that is in the name of Jesus causes us to speak out of a whole new dimension of the Spirit as He gives us the miraculous utterance of "new tongues." The name of Jesus is power against the deadly bite of a serpent, or the poisons that may exist in food or water. In Jesus' name we lay hands on the sick and they must recover. Why do miracles follow those that believe? Because the salvation that God has sent us to preach delivers men from every oppressing and evil thing. It's the name of Jesus that possesses all authority and in His name the gospel must be preached.

The miracles that come by the name of Jesus were observed throughout the book of Acts. When Philip held an evangelistic meeting in Samaria, the power that is in the name of Jesus was at work, for the unclean spirits cried out with a loud voice and came out of those who were possessed by them. Paul spoke in the name of Jesus when he encountered a woman with a familiar spirit, saying: "I command you in the name of Jesus Christ, come out of her;" and the demon left.[89] When Paul was building a fire after having been shipwrecked on the island of Malta, a deadly snake bit him; and the authority that Jesus had prescribed kept him from suffering any harm.[90] The poisons in nature are all part of a demon-cursed world, and Jesus came to destroy every influence of Satan. The power and authority that is in His name destroys the strongholds and effects of Satan, wherever they are and in whatever form they are encountered.

The new tongues that have been given were poured out on the day that the church was born. The language of the Spirit is the Holy Ghost testifying that Jesus has been crowned with all authority. It is the sign of the New Covenant – a miracle work of grace of the baptism of the Spirit and fire. Through this special gift, the saints are empowered to speak as the Holy Ghost addresses the Father.[91] The miraculous utterance of the Spirit is the proof that the Holy Spirit was poured out. Every time the language of the Spirit is heard, a testimony is given of the exalted Christ. The new tongues given by the name of Jesus is the evidence that the new teacher has come to lead us and to guide us. The gift of tongues was proof that the Spirit was poured out on both the Jews and the Gentiles. It is the evidence that Jesus has been given all power and authority, glorified and exalted. When He purged us of our sins, He sat down at the right hand of God and poured out the rivers of the gift of God. The gift of tongues was for all men everywhere, for the Spirit was poured out upon all flesh. The gift of tongues was established as a part of every local church so that Jesus would be glorified, and it was a boast of the Apostle Paul's spiritual life.[92]

The authority of the name of Jesus releases Heaven upon every person's soul. Wherever men call upon the name of Jesus, His miracles are present. Through mighty signs and wonders, the believer testifies of the name that has all power. The church will never be about what man can do, but rather what God will do through those who will believe. It's the name of Jesus that must be glorified and God has established His works in the midst of His church to glorify that name. These things that God has established by the name of Jesus exist for every generation and will not pass away for any reason.[93]

Faith that is by the Name

Peter's and John's understanding of the use of the name of Jesus was demonstrated when they commanded the lame man to walk. The authority of Christ Jesus that they had been eyewitnesses of for more than three years was still present and released through them as they spoke in the name of Jesus Christ of Nazareth. It was not just a delegated authority that they used, but rather authority and power that was resident in the name itself. Peter said that it was by the Name and through faith in the Name that the crippled man had received power to walk (Acts 3:16; 4:10). Jesus told His disciples that whatever they asked in His name, He would do it (John 14:13-14; 15:16; 16:23). They were not just asking in His name – they were speaking in His name and the results were the same as if Jesus had been standing there. The name of Jesus gave them the ability to function in divine authority and it is by that name that we to can do these works.

When God revealed His name to Moses, miracles commenced that had never been seen before. Moses went to the greatest kingdom on Earth and through the revelation of the name of God, he spoke and creation turned to his defense to fight against those who refused to obey the word of the Lord. Signs and wonders that were never seen before began to take place through the one who knew the name. Water was turned to blood, darkness was over the face of the Earth and hailstones burned with fire. The strongholds of a world of darkness that had opposed the things of God were subdued by the one who was sent.

By the name of God's Holy Child Jesus, great miracles are revealed as God stretches forth His hand to perform signs and wonders. Great boldness is imparted as every hindrance to the gospel is thrown down through the name of the One who reigns on High (Acts 4:30). Jesus manifested the Father's name in all of the works of power that He did (John 17:6,26). Today, His saints reveal the name of Jesus through mighty signs and wonders that He does through us. This authority in the name of Jesus gives witness that God has raised Him from the dead and set Him at His own right hand.

The Authority of the Blood of Jesus

We must believe that we have the right to stand before God as His ministers, otherwise we will never walk in the authority that is ours. If we think that we are still in some measure unacceptable to God, we will draw back from our position of authority in Christ Jesus. The blood of Jesus must be the cure for all of our sin and offense and supply us with the miracle of change. That change must be a cleansing of ourselves; a conscience void of offense, cleansed by the blood of Christ. We cannot stand before God in shame and iniquity– the blood of Jesus Christ is the only remedy. Sin produces separation from God and only faith in the blood removes it.

Thousands responding to the good new of the Gospel!

Fellowship with God is interrupted by a sense of sin, but faith in the blood is the cure. Boldness to come in before His presence, knowing that we are pure and free from all of our sins, is ours when we have to deal with any opposing circumstance. The authority of the blood that takes away sin and stops the powers of darkness must first be applied and believed on by each person before each one can be a minister of God. We must be willing to be convinced by the faith of God that the same authority of the blood that gives us access to the throne room of the Most High is equally our assurance that we have the right to expect the things that the Bible describes. The blood is our assurance that all of our petitions have been granted and whatever we ask Him, He will do.[94]

The blood of Jesus represents the whole life of Jesus. When we apply His blood we apply His whole life to ours. Christ Jesus took our place on the cross that we might take His place with Him in the throne room of Heaven. The blood of Jesus is our evidence that we no longer live! We are crucified with Christ and we are now in Him and He is in us; this is faith in the blood that results in an unshakable authority from God.

Apply the Blood of Jesus

"And by Him reconciled all things unto Himself, making peace through the blood of His cross, whether they be upon the Earth or in the heavens."

Colossians 1:20

The two most powerful forces that we are given are the name of Jesus and the blood of Jesus. When we pray in the name of Jesus and by the blood of Jesus, we pray on the basis of the highest authority that exists. We have the authority to apply the blood of Jesus to every situation in which Christ Jesus applied His blood – and we can expect the same results. When His blood was applied to sin, it was removed; therefore we can be confident that when we apply His blood to sin, then it must go as well.[95] It was the blood of Jesus that broke the power and effect of Satan's dominion over us; when Satan would attempt to enforce his will upon us, it is the authority of the blood that demands that he take his hands off of the property of God.[96] The blood of Jesus destroyed every power of the demonic realm. Through the death of Jesus and the blood of His cross, Satan's power was destroyed, and all of his host was stripped of their abilities to command the actions of men. Through the blood of Jesus, death was abolished, the law of sin and death were broken, and light and immortality were brought to light. When we apply the blood of Jesus against any work or activity of Satan, it renders every demonic power completely powerless.

From the field of the National Stadium, Kathmandu, Nepal.

The blood of Jesus is the boundary between Heaven and hell. There is no power of hell that has the right to cross this boundary of God's redemption and protection. When Jesus stripped all principalities and powers of their authority, He did so by His death on the cross.[97] The blood of the cross is therefore both our reminder and theirs – that they have no right to afflict or torment those who have been redeemed by the blood. We have the double cure for sin and disease; we must have confidence that what God has supplied is remedy enough for all we need – just have faith in His blood.[98] We all must proclaim loudly, "Redeemed, redeemed by the blood of the Lamb!" Satanic powers would attempt to impose their will upon the people of God;–although they have no right to violate the blood barrier, unless the saints of God stand up and take the authority that has been given, they will overrun the absence of such authority and impose what they have no right to do!

Sins Washed Away

"Who shall accuse God's elect? God makes us righteous."
Romans 8:33

The blood of Jesus gives us the authority to come into the presence of God and stand before the throne of grace. Are you washed in the blood – in the soul-cleansing blood of the Lamb? Are your garments spotless – are they whiter than snow? Are you washed in the blood of the Lamb? There is no power that can wash away sins other than the blood of Jesus Christ. If we accept what Jesus has done for us through the blood of the cross, then we can know that all of our sins have been washed away and that we stand spotless before the Lord.[99] We have been given authority to boldly proclaim that sin is completely removed by the blood of Jesus Christ.[100] There is no other remedy for sin and death, only the blood of Jesus. Anyone who takes the blood of Jesus for their cleansing from sin has been given the authority to walk in the purity of God and union with

Jesus Christ. By the authority of the blood, Satan has no right to accuse us.[101] If we sin, the authority of the blood provides us with the power to be cleansed from any sin that we may commit. Although God has made a way that we should never sin again; if we sin we have an unlimited supply that will cleanse us from all sin.

New believers worshipping the Lord.

As the Mediator and the One who testifies of the power of redemption, Jesus forever lives to make intercession for us.[102] He is our Advocate with the Father who is faithful and just to cleanse us from all unrighteousness through the blood that He has poured out. Therefore no one can lay any charge to God's elect, for it is Christ Jesus who has made us righteous by His own blood. When we stand before the highest seat of judgment, we are found faultless and blameless because of the blood. One of the questions that we must deal with is: do we agree with His judgment concerning those who have been washed in the blood of the Lamb? Do we believe that such life and purity has been provided through the blood of God? God has made everyone who will believe righteous by the blood of Jesus.[103] Through the blood we are no longer common or unclean.[104] It is His judgment that through the blood of the everlasting covenant every stain of sin is removed and the soul and spirit of man is made pure and holy. The testimony of God to us is simply, "Come let us reason together, though your sins be as scarlet – they shall be white like wool; though they be like crimson, they will be whiter than snow"[105].

The Ability to Repent

"When they heard this they were silenced and glorified God, saying, "Well then, unto the Gentiles also God has granted repentance unto life."

Acts 11:18

Repentance only works when the blood of Jesus is applied. Without the blood of Jesus, a person can be sorry all day long for his wrongdoing, but it will accomplish him nothing. The deep desire to have a change of life and do what is good and pleasing in God's sight can neither remove the penalty of death, nor change the nature of a man. Repentance is only granted through the death of Christ Jesus, who bore our sins away at Calvary. He is the One who tasted death for every man, and bore our sins in His own body on the tree. Only through His blood can His life now be supplied. Without the shedding of the blood of Jesus, man is still subject to the law of sin and death. [106] The blood of the Old Testament offerings could offer a substitute until the Seed should come – the Lamb, the offering of which all those sacrifices testified. Now their value is lost forever, for the fullness of time has come; the offering was prepared and Christ Jesus was crucified. All the Old Testament offerings were only like a play pointing to the offering God Himself would make – offerings which have now been done away with since His blood has now been given. Now when His blood is applied to a repentant heart, that repentance brings a change and the power of the life of Christ is imparted. We have been liberated from the curse of sin and death by the blood of our Passover Lamb.[107] The sins of all mankind have been sent away, and the testimony of that sin and its penalty of death have been removed from before the presence of God forever.[108] We now have the commission and authority to command all men everywhere to repent and to turn to the Living God. The gift of repentance has been granted to us with all its rights and benefits by the blood and through the name of Jesus.[109]

Equally, God, who loves the whole world, has no opportunity to forgive anyone without the application of the blood of Jesus. Through Jesus Christ alone has forgiveness of sins been granted. There may be many good people in the religions of the world who sincerely seek God's forgiveness, but their religions have no authority to grant forgiveness; for that power can only be found in the blood of the Lamb, Christ Jesus. The blood of Jesus must be applied if the stain of sin that pollutes the soul and spirit is to be removed. It does not matter whether one is a Jew or Gentile, without applying the blood that was shed for the sins of the people there is no remission of their sins. The only sacrifice that matters, the sacrifice that forever provides a cleansing from all sin – is the blood of Jesus. If we refuse this redeeming sacrifice, and if we do not take His blood and apply it to our lives, then we will die in our sins; and eternal death will be the consequence. If we take His blood and confess our sins, He is just and faithful to cleanse us from all unrighteousness. Confession alone cannot do it, and even a sorrowful and contrite heart comes up short; but when the blood of Jesus is applied, every sin and every one of its effects are forever removed.

The Altar of God

"The word of the cross is to them that perish foolishness, but to us who are saved the power of God."

1 Corinthians 1:18

The one thing that represents the Gospel of Jesus Christ more than anything else is the cross. We must recognize that when we speak of the cross of Christ we are referring to that altar on which the blood of Jesus was offered.[110] What was purchased for us on the cross was purchased by His shed blood. The preaching of the cross is the power of God and the power of the New Covenant because it is where the blood of Jesus was supplied. It does not matter who you are; whether you are a Jew or a Gentile there is only one way to be changed and brought into relationship with God and that is through the cross of Christ.[111] If this redeeming work is emphasized – if Christ Jesus is lifted up in those things which we proclaim, then all men will be drawn to Him.[112] It is by faith in the blood that we have faith to see the lost saved. Faith in the blood gives us faith to break every stronghold of Satan and chain of addiction.

The authority of the cross is witnessed through our lives because we are crucified with Him. By the miracle of salvation His death became our death so that His life might be our life. The blood of the cross has become our testimony of a redeemed and transformed life. It is the token of our new life that we now live by the power that is in His blood. At the cross, where the bread of life was broken and the cup of communion was supplied, the veil between Earth and Heaven was ripped in two;

and all who would believe are invited to come and step inside. [113] It was at the cross that the fountain of redeeming blood was poured out to supply a cleansing now and forever for all who put their trust in Him.

Believing on the Lord Jesus Christ

In the cross we see how Father feels about sin and His demand that it be put to death. Who can begin to comprehend the travail of Father's heart at the sufferings of Jesus on the cross and also His ecstatic joy that redemption's price had paid our access back to Him. [114] It is through the cross that we can comprehend how desperately God loves us, for it is here that He gave His Only Begotten Son so that if anyone would believe they could be saved. In knowing that He spared not His own Son to redeem us, we can be certain that He will continue to do for us what no other power can do. [115] We may be confident that Father will freely give us all things that belong to the authority and power of Heaven! It is in the cross that we should gain great confidence with God, for here we were released from everything that could stop the abundance of God's blessings, authority and dominion in our life. Therefore we may boldly proclaim, "If God be for us, who can be against us!"

Through treasuring the cross and laying down our lives, God's glory is revealed in us. If we are to follow Him in all of His power and authority, then we must deny ourselves so that the life of Christ Jesus might be seen. The great exchange took place on Calvary's hill, Christ Jesus took our place to die for all our sins that we might take His place in standing before men with all Heaven's glory and authority. Our confession and manner of life must be, "I am crucified with Christ and Christ now lives, not me."[116] Our judgment must be just and reasonable that if Christ Jesus died for all then all are dead, and that we should from this time forth only live for Him.[117] When we live for Him, then it is that same Jesus that will be seen – the One who caused the blind to see and lived in oneness with the Father in unlimited glory.

Communion through the Blood

"For this is My blood of the New Testament, which is poured out for many for the removal of sins."

Matthew 26:28

Through death, the Lord Jesus poured out the power of our communion. His blood supplied us with an unlimited forgiveness – not only for our sins, but also for the sins of the whole world.[118] His body and blood are the elements of His sacrifice for our sins. It was not just by His life that we live, but also by His death. For the New Covenant is established by the death of the testator, and remission of sins is granted through the blood, which represents His death.[119] When we consider the activity of communion in which we partake of these tokens of the blood and body of Jesus, we are testifying of our personal application of His blood to our lives and of our faith in the blood of Jesus.[120] Through His blood, we are granted repentance and are forgiven of our sins. Through His blood we are made a new creation in which Christ Jesus lives and dwells. Through the body of His flesh we are presented holy, unrebukable, and unreprovable because all our offenses have been removed.[121] Communion is a testimony of the blood of Jesus being applied to our lives. It testifies that we are daily living by His blood and body. We apply His blood to everything that is dead and it lives, everything that is wrong so that it may be made right, and all trespasses and offenses so that we may forgive just like we are forgiven. Jesus who is faithful and just to forgive us of our sins and to cleanse us from all unrighteousness by His blood supplies us with the same ability to forgive and show mercy to everyone else as well.[122]

We must recognize that all of our communion and fellowship with God is found only in the body and blood of Jesus. When we worship or when we pray, any interaction that we have with God is through the body and blood of Jesus. Our participation in the communion (of eating and drinking the elements that represent His body and blood) is an acknowledgement of the means by which we were made acceptable to God, and are allowed to enter into His Holy Presence. Therefore, just as the High Priest would take the blood of the sacrifice and come into the Holy of Holies, we take the blood of Jesus in our day-to-day and minute-by-minute interaction with Him, and come with all boldness into the Holiest place of all.

When we partake of the juice that represents the blood of Jesus, we are testifying of how the life of Jesus came into us. We are testifying of how our sins were washed away and how they are removed (if we commit such an act again). When we partake of communion, it is a testimony of how we were sprinkled with the blood and brought into the relationship of the New Covenant, which takes away sin and creates the life of Jesus within us.[123] It is the testimony of how He dwells in us and how we dwell in Him and live by Him.[124] Just as in the first Passover in which the blood was applied to the house of those who put their trust in God's salvation, the blood of Jesus, our Passover Lamb, is applied to our lives – and we continually live in Him and by His blood.[125]

Jesus served this communion to His disciples, and established the practice of the communion service when He said: "This is my body, take it and eat it," and "This is the blood of the new covenant; drink it all."[126] This was not to be done just once, but often. Unlike the Passover celebration which took place only once a year, this communion was to be continually observed. Although there was no clear definition of how often this kind of communion service should take place, Paul simply said that as often as you do it you show His death until He comes.[127] The larger issue that must be understood is our need to recognize that communion extends beyond the table of a communion service, and it is a token and a reminder of how we are to continually live. It sets the tone for the quality and intimacy of our interaction with Christ Jesus. The life of Jesus and His blood are inseparable, and all our life in God is found in oneness with the Lord.[128] Just as Jesus lived by His union with the Father, we live by our union with Jesus. Our union with and through the life of Christ Jesus was made possible by His blood, and by our reception of it and faith in it.[129]

The Authority of the Covenant

The blood is the means by which the New Covenant was established and therefore it is the authority of the covenant. A covenant is a contract that is the testimony of the agreed upon relationship between all parties involved. It is the authority that describes the obligations and interactions of all those involved in the agreement. Every part of the covenant functions by the power of the blood. God has provided for us a means by which every claim of sin and death can be removed. Every power of Satan, sickness, and death can be broken by the means of this blood-covenant. The authority of the covenant is based upon the power of the One who made it to enforce its privileges, protection, and blessings. There is no power in Heaven or on Earth that can ever revoke the authority of the blood of Jesus. It is for this reason that we sing,

Would you be free from your burden of sin?
There is power in the blood, power in the blood.
Would you over evil the victory win?
There's wonderful power in the blood.
Would you do service for Jesus your King?
There is wonderful power in the blood.

It is through the blood that we are supplied with all the provision, protection and perfection of Heaven. The blood is the power and authority of every dimension of our life in God. When the blood of Jesus is applied, the Holy Spirit comes rushing in, and all of Heaven is mobilized. There is no power in Heaven, or in Earth, or under the Earth that can stand against the authority of the blood of Jesus. Throughout the ages to come, all mankind will sing songs of praise for the blood of Jesus. Every tribe and every tongue, kindred, and nation will lift their voice in praise to the One who redeemed us with His own blood.

Our lives are bound together with Jesus through the blood of the everlasting covenant. Through this covenant we have been made bone of His bone and flesh of His flesh. Through the blood of the covenant, His nature and identity were imparted into us. In every generation, both in the Old Covenant and the New Covenant, God made provision to dwell with man through the blood of the covenant. All of those sacrifices from Abel until Jesus only represented God's true redeeming sacrifice: the Word made flesh, the Lamb of God to take away our sins. The blood of God is applied to our hearts so that we might become His temple. The blood which He gave was a purchase in full for the spirit, soul and body of men that are now made one with Him. The blood of the New Covenant is the final and everlasting covenant of God with man. There will never be any other remedy for mens' sins and no other means of access to God. The central theme of all of man's interaction with God is the blood of the covenant, and through His blood we forever dwell in Him. Ten trillion years from now, we will still be singing out:

Redeemed, Redeemed, Redeemed by the blood of the Lamb!

Eternal Redemption

"Neither by the blood of goats and calves, but by with His own blood He entered once into the Holy Place: having obtained eternal redemption for us."

Hebrews 9:12

The blood of Jesus that is presented to us by Jesus, our great High Priest, must produce certainty and confidence about our relationship with God, and authority over all things that would oppose us. Out of this certainty and confidence, an absolute authority will arise within us to crush every scorpion and serpent, and every power of sin and the demonic realm. In this authority, no power of darkness can harm us, and every demon is subject to us. Every mouth is stopped and every power of condemnation is silenced when the blood of Jesus Christ is applied. If we apply the blood of the covenant properly, then we will apply it with faith and authority: knowing that nothing is more powerful than the sacrifice that Jesus made. Our confidence in the blood of Jesus causes us to know that what God has promised is ours today, that the power of the blood covenant cannot pass away. Through this we refuse all intimidation, and with the authority that the Spirit of the Lord commands, we speak and everything must obey. It was with this confidence and authority that Jesus entered into Heaven with His own blood to obtain an eternal redemption. It is with this same confidence and authority that He has entrusted unto us the ability to minister in His place, as priests of our great High Priest, Christ Jesus.

The blood of the Passover lamb was applied to every house of God's covenant people in Egypt that first Passover night. Death could not trespass against the blood and claim the lives of those who were under its protection; for wherever the blood is applied, there the power of redemption and the power of God's life resides.[130] It is the sacrifice for sin that stops the plague and provides deliverance from every curse and claim of Satan.[131] The power of the blood of Jesus can never pass away. It is more effective than those sacrifices that were only representative. It's not our houses that have been sprinkled with His blood today. It's not the blood of an animal sacrifice that has been applied to our lives, for we were sprinkled with His blood; it is on us now.

[132] Our great High Priest has applied it to our lives.[133] Its undiminishing power will never pass away, it's a covenant that is just as effective today as when it poured from Emmanuel's veins at Calvary. Now as His priests, we present His blood to all who would be saved.[134] We apply it as the cure for sin, for sickness, and for disease. In every way that the blood of the Old Covenant was used, we apply the blood of Jesus just the same today. With the word of authority and a command in Jesus' name, the blood takes hold of all who will believe – and everything unlike God must flee away.

Heaven's Currency

Heaven's currency, the currency that purchased us, was the blood of Jesus. We were not redeemed with corruptible things like silver and gold, but by the precious blood of Jesus, as a Lamb without spot or blemish. A value was placed upon the soul of man, and the price was the blood of Jesus. There was no power that could break the Satanic claim other than the blood of the Redeemer. The blood is the evidence and token of the life that contained it, its value only equal to the value of the One who shed it and its authority only as powerful as the One from whom it came. The One who had all authority and had created everything was able to break every unholy claim with the power of His blood. His life was more powerful than death, His righteousness more powerful than sin and His love able to liberate those imprisoned in hate. The power of sin, and all its twisted desire, was erased by the righteousness of God and through His divine nature. The Father's devotion and jealous love, with all of Heaven's power and authority, will work to ensure that the power of the blood of His precious Son is enforced. God, who paid such a high price for our sins to be washed away, will most certainly enforce the results of that price! God purchased us, so we are His, and in His jealous love He watches over us to perform His word.

Thousands respond to the gospel invitation!

Jesus purchased the church with His own blood. All that has been purchased by the blood of Jesus belongs to Father. The price He paid is the measure of how valuable we are to Him. Nothing can possibly be more sacred and precious to the Father than the life and blood of Jesus. We must be careful to understand the sacredness and power of the blood of Jesus, lest we should count the blood of the covenant as some unholy thing, misuse it, and end up walking over that sacred thing by which we have been redeemed. The blood of Jesus must become as sacred to us as it is to the Father, lest we outrage the Holy Spirit. When the blood of Jesus is given its proper place in our thoughts and actions, then we will discover more fully the life-giving authority that was granted unto us. The life of Jesus was poured out so that the fullness of the life of God might be poured into us. His blood is the sum total of His life, and we now live by Him.

The Love

To dwell in the love of God is to dwell in God. To know the love of Christ that passes knowledge is to be filled with all the fullness of God. The love of God was defined in the way that Christ laid down His life for us. It was defined in the cross, where Jesus bore our sins and tasted death for every man. God commended His love towards us, and Christ died for us, while we were yet sinners. Now He will all the more freely give us all things by Him, and of this we must be confident. We are freely supplied with every dimension of God's grace, power and authority, and we can be confident that there is nothing that God has promised that He will fail to do.

Through His love, He gave His life as a ransom for us. God so loved us that He spared not His own Son in order to win us, and as we engage in His affairs, contending for the souls of men, every dimension of the power of the kingdom will be seen. The blood is the testimony and the proof of God's great love and unlimited commitment to give us all things. The blood of Jesus is the most precious subject in the bible. It was poured out to us through the deepest affections of God's love for us, and it is released through our lives to a lost and dying world through the same compassion. He did all these wonderful things for us so that that He might bring many sons into glory through the blood of His sacrifice.

Healing in the Blood

The blood of Jesus will always and forever retain the healing power and cure for all of man's sin and disease; it will never lose its power. Those who take hold of faith in the blood of Jesus are given the authority to execute the double cure that flowed from Emmanuel's veins. The One who has cleansed all our iniquities is also the One who has healed all our diseases and pains. Jesus bore our sins in his body on the tree so that we might have the authority and ability to live unto righteousness (the life of God); by His stripes we were healed. Our authority is found in our confidence that these things are absolutely true! And therefore, we insist upon them and will not have it any other way. When we stand up to proclaim this good news, we do so in the power of the cross. Our divine commission is to proclaim what the cross of Christ has purchased. We can be certain that with this proclamation the authority and power of God will be revealed.

The Authority of Sonship

"But to as many as received, to them He gave authority to be sons of God even to as many as would believe upon His name."

John 1:12

There could be no greater honor than to be born into the family of God and called a son. Yet we are not just called sons, but also given the authority of the Son, Christ Jesus. We now have the same authority that Jesus has over all the powers of darkness and every physical and natural element. A new dimension of faith has been unveiled, the faith to function as a son. Jesus came and demonstrated the authority of the Son, with all power and authority. It was seen in Him that which the psalmist described: "For you have made Him a little lower than the angels and have crowned Him with glory and honor. You made Him to have dominion over the works of Your hand and You put all things under His feet" (Psalm 8:4-6; Hebrews 2:6-8).

Though the prophets of old were mighty in their exploits, they could not attain to the status of a son. Moses was used like no other, but he could not boast of such a right. Though Abraham was the father of faith, he had to wait until the promise was fulfilled and Jesus came and purchased our redemption before he would be a son. Through redemption, what God had formed Adam to be was restored to man again. A spiritual resurrection took place by the Spirit of the Lord, and we were given the power to live as one with Jesus Christ the Son.

In Christ Jesus we have this unspeakable gift. His Son is now revealed in us through this great salvation. Now, in the greatness of God's own good pleasure, which has been given unto us, and through the greatness of His love, we are called the sons of God (1 John 3:1). Sonship is the gift of the new creation that we receive when we are born again through the One who transformed our lives. When we have received what He has freely given, then we are born as the sons of God. We are not just subjects of His kingdom, nor are we only friends, but we are sons: those begotten of the Father. He has not just given us a position, but His authority, the authority of a fully matured son. The only issue now is: who will believe our report that they might live by the faith of Jesus Christ?

Christ's Sonship

"Therefore, you are no longer a servant but a son, and if a son then also an heir of God through Christ."

Galatians 4:7

A child has limited authority in the Father's house and is no different from a servant when it comes to having the right to make decisions. However, once the child matures and steps into the appointed role as the heir, then as the son he is the recognized owner and functions with the same authority that belongs to his Father. It is this authority that Paul refers to in Galatians 4:7 – the authority of sonship (hiouthesia) that belongs to all New Testament saints. We are no longer to act as mere children in Father's house, but as matured sons! Through the power of the Holy Ghost we are given the ability and insight to function as those who are of full age. Through the faith of Jesus Christ we are called to take our position of authority over the things that we have inherited in our Father's house.

Why would we draw back through unbelief and take less of a

position than the one Father desires for us to have? We must be willing to believe what God has said and step up boldly into the responsibility that He has given. Unfortunately, many are fearful to take such a step; many are more comfortable living as a child. To many, the idea of sonship seems to be more than just an unspeakable gift; it seems to be one that is unthinkable. For many, the joys, benefits and blessings of faith are placed somewhere in the future and the life of Christ only religiously pursued. Imprisoned by religious ritual, the gospel is modified and tailored to fit more comfortably to each person's strengths and abilities. John Wesley, reflecting on this verse, spoke of his life that had been bound by his religious beliefs, saying, "I had even then the faith of a servant, though not that of a son" (Journal [London, 1872], I, 76n.).

Pastor Mark preaching the good news.

Sonship is only understood in the context of the life of Christ Jesus. Jesus, as the only begotten Son, showed us how to walk as the sons of God and do the works of the Father. It was not a position given only to an elect few, but a call to everyone who would believe. Anyone, both then and now, whoever will receive, to them He has given the authority to be the sons of God.[135] The Spirit of the Son testifies of this and cries out within our hearts saying, "Abba Father."[136] Why should it matter what we want when God wants to crown us with His glory and show the world that we are co-inheritors with Christ. There is no room for another classification of Christian; there are only those who are in Christ and those who are not, and those who are in Christ are sons and heirs of God![137]

The only way the life and ministry of Jesus will be realized in our lives is for each one of us to believe what God has said and then begin to live it! Through the confessions of our mouths and the actions of our life, we must resolve ourselves to be that which God described. To demand it our own way and refuse to accept what God has provided for us to be can only be classified as, at best, unbelief. To hide behind our own ideas and to cowardly retreat to the dens of our own beliefs and then proclaim that we are doing the will of the Father is make-believe. The Word of God calls us all to come forward – to believe and receive what God has freely given. We have been given the life of the Spirit so that we can walk in God's divine glory and power. The proof that Jesus has been raised from the dead and has sat down at the Father's right hand is revealed through the sons that He has brought into this glory. Will we refuse Gods plan and opt out of such authority and responsibility? We have been invited into a fellowship with Jesus and given an opportunity to enjoy His relationship with the Father so that all men might know that we are the sons of God. [138] It is this relationship that we were born into when we were born of His Spirit. Come, let us walk in the Spirit so that the life of Christ Jesus the Son may be revealed in us.

New converts in Nepal!

The Glory of the Son

"In bringing many sons into glory it was appropriate for Him (for whom and by whom all things are) that the Captain of their salvation should be made perfect through suffering."

Hebrews 2:10

Behold, what manner of love the Father has bestowed on us; look at what the Captain of our salvation has done! He has brought us into sonship, an inheritance beyond what we could ever ask or think. A whole new dimension of faith is now revealed to the sons of men; we are heirs of God joined together with the One who suffered for our sins, Christ Jesus the Only Begotten Son!

Jesus has brought us into His own glory.[139] He has given us the glory that the Father gave to Him. By His own great power, through His own good pleasure, He has made us like His Son. We may say that we are not of this world, but that as He is, so are we now in this world today.[140] We are transformed and transfigured by this work of grace, but if we are going to walk in the authority and power of it we must believe God's report. This is the record that God has given of His Son: the One who has the Son has life – the life of God in us![141] We walk in Him and live in Him and we are empowered and immersed with His identity.[142]

Pastor Mark and Sudip ministering the good news of the Gospel!

Each one of us must be willing to be conformed to the image of the Son, who is the express image of the Father. We are to understand that God has chosen to reveal His Son in us; this is the faith that now has been spoken into our hearts by the Word of God.[143] We are to believe what God has done and be conformed to the image of His Son, so that it might be shown that Christ Jesus is the firstborn among many brethren.[144] We must be willing to accept this grace that has provided oneness with both Jesus and the Father so that the world may know that the Father sent Jesus.[145] There is boldness and glory that we must allow to arise and shine through our lives, boldness and glory that only comes by the willingness to step out in sonship faith. As the sons of God, we must be willing to follow Jesus into every dimension of His authority – not in a different way than He has modeled for us in Matthew, Mark, Luke and John, but in the same display of Father's will being done through our lives.

Manifested Sons

"For the creation eagerly awaits the manifestation of the sons of God."

Romans 8:19

The ministry of sonship has begun. As the sons of God we are taught by the Holy Spirit how to function in the power and authority that Christ Jesus now has; to do His works and greater works, and to set the captives free. Although all this fullness is available, there is still more to being sons than what we can have right now. The full revelation of all that God has made us to be will not be manifested until we receive a glorified body.[146] When we put on our resurrected body we will see Him as He is, for we shall be like Him. When we step into that heavenly tabernacle and then ultimately into the resurrected body, a whole new dimension of sonship will begin.[147] J.B. Phillips put it well when He translated <u>Romans 8:19</u>,"The whole creation is on tiptoe to see the wonderful sight of the sons of God coming into their own" (Mounce, p. 184). Although we are not yet in this unspeakable glorified state, we are still the sons of God with the authority of the Son: Christ Jesus. There is a great liberating work that must be done right now so that men might be saved. If we walk in the Spirit and live in the Spirit, then the glory of sonship will be seen and the benefits of this abundant life enjoyed.[148]

Jesus is the model of sonship. We must walk in His footsteps if we expect to live His life![149] As the Son, Jesus brought many sons into this glory, and showed us by example the kind of life that we must have. The only way to live the life that we have been called to is to imitate God and do what Jesus did.[150] Jesus showed us how to live the heavenly life (the life of doing the Father's will), and He showed us how creation would be liberated through the ministry of the Son. He came to set men free from the bondage of darkness, and to bring all who would believe into His glorious liberty. All creation now waits for the day when it will be liberated from the influences of Satan, and experience the glorious liberty of the sons of God. When God creates a new Heaven and a new Earth, all creation will be affected, and everything in it will be instantly changed. In that day, all creation will be liberated from every evil effect of sin and death.[151]

However, we must recognize that the time of the reign of Christ has already begun. As His representatives, we have been commanded to proclaim the liberating, conquering power of the Spirit that is found only in Jesus' Name! Wherever the gospel is preached, creation (and especially men) will experience the benefits of the presence of the Lord. The glorious liberty of the sons of God, which is found in the Holy Spirit, has authority over the curse of sin, sickness, disease, pestilence, and all oppression. Every spiritual blessing that is in Heaven belongs to those who will believe; they will have power over all the works of the devil, his curse, and poverty. When the gospel is preached, it is a joyful sound. When those who have the authority of the Son proclaim the gospel, the creation is set free. The prophet Isaiah described the effect of the sons of God (the redeemed) upon creation when he said, "They will go out with joy and be led forth with peace, and all of the mountains and the hills shall break forth before you into singing, and all the trees of the field shall clap their hands" (Isaiah 55:12). When the glorious liberty of salvation is experienced, then sorrow, sighing, and mourning must flee away.[152] What a glorious time we live in, for the reign of Christ Jesus has begun!

The Authority of Faith

"And Jesus said unto them, Because of your unbelief: for verily I say unto you, If ye have faith as a grain of mustard seed, ye shall say unto this mountain, Remove hence to yonder place; and it shall remove; and nothing shall be impossible unto you."

Matthew 17:20

Theologians and laymen alike have given many definitions of faith, but none should mean as much to us as the one that Jesus gave. Jesus did not define faith as a religious belief or an ideology; He defined faith as the supernatural authority of God released through those who would believe.[153] Faith is not what a person thinks about life or God, but it is the power of God at work in us by the Holy Spirit. Faith is miracle-working power that produces the miraculous life of Jesus. Faith is the power to move mountains and command sycamine trees to be planted in the sea. The authority of faith is the power that enables the son of God to command the winds and the waves and have them obey.[154] Those who function in faith receive the dead to life again, and command the moon and the sun to stand still in the sky. By faith a nation passed through the Red Sea and the walls of Jericho came down. The authority of God's word produces the power of faith in those who will believe. Faith makes the invisible things visible, and creates everything from those things that are unseen. Through faith kingdoms are subdued, righteousness is worked, promises obtained, the mouths of lions are stopped, the violence of fire is quenched, men escape the edge of the sword, are made strong out of weakness, wax valiant in fight, and turn the armies of the enemies to flight.[155] Faith is the authority of God displayed in acts of power!

There were many great signs and wonders done by faith, but the greatest miracle of faith is the power that changed man's hearts. By faith a new heart and a new spirit were created, and the bodies of men were made the temples of the Holy Ghost! Through God's work of grace the word of faith became a part of our being and now resides in our hearts and mouths. From the word of faith we speak the Word of God and the Holy Spirit creates everything new. In our heart there is a belief and from our mouth there is a confession that brings forth righteousness and truth.[156]

Faith is the miraculous life of Christ in us. Faith is the abiding presence of the Father and the Holy Ghost in our lives. By the miracle of faith we were crucified with Christ and by the miracle of faith we were raised up together with Him. The word of faith that is in our mouth is, "I am crucified with Christ and it is no longer I that lives but Christ who lives in me. And the life that I now live I live by the faith of the Son of God who loved me and gave Himself for me."[157] The faith of God reproduced the life of Christ within us and gives to us the proofs that we are in Him and that He is in us.[158] We have His faith, not some faith of men; we have the faith of Jesus, God's faith by the Holy Ghost. We have the miraculous life of divine union with God and in this we discover the authority of faith. Having received the same Spirit of faith we now speak. When we speak we do not speak out of our own beliefs, instead we speak those things that God has spoken.[159] It is Christ who speaks the word of faith in us by the Holy Spirit.

Great Faith

Jesus' definition of faith was characterized in the confidence that a Roman Centurion had in Him. The centurion recognized who Jesus was, and laid hold on the power and authority which Jesus possessed. The centurion was in such awe of Jesus that he did not feel worthy to even have Him come to his house. The centurion's faith was born in His awe for Jesus. The centurion, so captivated by the person of Jesus, was certain that He could do anything. The centurion saw in Jesus the greatness of a kingdom that was greater than Rome and knew that the authority of Jesus was absolute. The centurion did not need much from the King of kings, he only needed Jesus to speak the word and he knew that he would have the things he needed. The centurion did not need to be convinced because the Living Word, Christ Jesus, had already captivated his heart. The centurion only needed to hear this One of great authority "speak the word" and he knew it would be done. He needed no other proof, his eyes did not need to see the miracle because the word of authority was enough for him to call it done. Jesus said, "this is it; this is the faith!" Jesus was calling to every generation declaring, "this is how it works!" He said, "I have not found so great of faith in Israel" (Matthew 8:10).

The authority of the word, and our willingness to accept it and act on it, is a theme that runs throughout the scripture. To move in this faith, we must be struck with awe at the power of God who has authority to do anything He chooses. We must hear His word telling us that He cares for us, and that He will do whatever we ask. In knowing Jesus and the authority of His word we can call it done![160] We have been given the unlimited provision of the Holy Spirit, a revelation of Jesus that the centurion could not have known. All we need to do is lift up our eyes towards Heaven and see Jesus. We must look unto the author and finisher of our faith and know and believe His love. When we look at him, our hearts will be filled with awe and we will have great confidence in His love. In this relationship of love, knowing how much He loves us, we will also know that He will do whatever we ask.

The centurion was not of the household of faith, and had no rights to the covenant or promises. He was from a pagan race that did not know God. He was a gentile oppressor, and that meant he was unclean to the Hebrew race. Even though Jesus was sent specifically to the lost sheep of the house of Israel, He still could not ignore this kind of faith. It was the kind of faith He had been looking for in Israel. It was the kind of faith that pleases God. He did not find it in Israel; he found it in a centurion's heart. Faith arose in the heart of this sinful man because he adored the Son. The centurion's faith created an access into the realms of the Kingdom that had not yet been made available to him. The centurion's faith, a faith that lays hold on the promises of God, removed the wait and he was immediately provided access and his petition was granted. Unlike those in Israel, the centurion did not have to wade through a myriad of doctrinal questions before he could believe. His eyes saw Jesus, and his heart was filled with love. He had a need, and his heart was filled with confidence that he would not be rejected. He knew that this loving Savior would respond to his request.

Today, if we will only have faith in God, God's faith will be released through us. If we will believe God, then we will see the great things that He has promised become a reality in our lives. If we will have faith that Jesus is exalted above all authorities, with everything subject to Him, then we can be certain that nothing can prevent what He has said. We can know and believe the love that God has for us and be filled with confidence that

He has accepted us and will grant our request. We can have the same confidence that the centurion had in the word of Christ. We do not have to wait until we can see it with our eyes in order to believe, because His word is evidence enough! Confidence in Christ Jesus and the assurance of His love will produce great faith. Your heart cannot condemn you when you know that His blood has made you right. The thoughts of rejection cannot withhold you when you gaze upon His love. The Living Word calls you and beckons everyone to come. "Have the faith of God," He says; now call it done. Don't hesitate – recognize who Jesus is and let Him meet your needs.

Faith Produces Miracles

A woman, in desperate need for her daughter to be healed, came to Jesus even though she had no right. In her initial interaction with Him it looked as though she would be rejected. This woman had a desperate need that compelled her to lay hold on eternal life. It did not matter what anyone said, she knew that Christ Jesus alone had her answer and the help that she needed. She came to Him and never took her eyes off the One who was the Savior of the world. Somehow, His love had seized her heart and she was able to realize that He could not refuse her request. His faith had captivated her and nothing could dissuade her. The harsh words that Jesus spoke would have caused others to be offended, but all it did for her was make her more determined. Her willingness to be broken and humble only ensured the answer to her request. The faith of Jesus that flowed out as he spoke about the children's bread caused her to realize that all she would need was a single crumb to work her miracle. She had no access to the promises; she was a Syrophoenician woman who was unclean, with a daughter who was demon possessed. How could she expect that Jesus would not just pass her by? When Jesus saw her faith, it could not be denied. It was the faith that God was looking for, the faith that would lay hold upon the Son. It was the faith that would acknowledge who Jesus was: the Savior of the world. All Jesus could say was, "woman, great is your faith" your daughter is made whole (<u>Matthew 15:28</u>).

So many come to Christ!

One of the Jesus' most radical statements produced one of the most radical displays of faith in the New Testament: "Jesus said to her, 'let the children be filled first: for it is not right to take the children's bread and throw it to the dogs'" (<u>Matthew 15:26</u>). One thing is for certain; this Gentile woman of Syrophoenicia had nothing in her theology that dissuaded her from believing in miracles. Her daughter was demon possessed, she was desperate, and Jesus was the Man of miracles. Jesus made this radical statement to define who His miracles were for, when He said: "[I]t's the children's bread." The children's bread belonged to those Israelites that God had made a covenant with, and this unclean woman had no right to eat it. However, this woman could hear the love of God, even in the harsh words, and found reason to hope in the possibility of a crumb. In her humility she behaved herself with the utmost respect, and Jesus said, because of what you have said, here is the children's bread, and she partook of what had not yet been made available to her race. Her faith in who Jesus was laid hold upon the miracle. It was a faith that worked in her by His love, and by her humility. It was a bold faith that could not be denied.

The Hearing of Faith

The Holy Spirit reveals the Word of God to us. If we will open up our eyes and look, then we will recognize that there is nothing that we could ask that He would refuse. The Holy Spirit not only reveals the word, but also speaks faith into our lives so that, by that faith, we may live in the supernatural supply of Heaven. When we behold the Word of God and are captivated by what is said, then the Spirit supplies the faith. When the word is mixed with faith, then we have all the promises of God. Some would argue for different kinds of faith; but in truth, there is only one kind of faith, and that is the faith that comes by the Word, Christ Jesus.

Faith produces different kinds of miracles, but there is only one kind of faith. The one kind of faith that we have received is God's faith, which is supplied to us by Jesus Christ and flows to us by the Holy Spirit.[161] The faith that is given to us by the Spirit is saving faith and miracle faith. This faith comes to us as the fruit of the Spirit, and as the gift of the Spirit. The person who works miracles by the Spirit through the hearing of faith also received salvation by the Spirit through the same faith.[162] Faith is the active agent by which the Holy Spirit produces the miracle in and through us. It's God's faith, the faith of Jesus Christ spoken into the lives of all who will believe. It is this faith that we are to contend for; the faith that was once delivered unto the saints. It is by this faith that we were born of God and it is by this faith that we are now perfected.[163] It is no less a miracle of faith to grow and mature into all the glorious things that God has chosen for us to be than it is to cast out devils and cure disease. All of these things happen by the working of the Holy Spirit through the activity of faith.

Paul speaks of faith as a unique manifestation of the Spirit, distinguishing it from miracles and gifts of healings.[164] It must be understood, however, that all miracles and gifts of healing take place by faith. It does not matter what gifts of the Spirit that we may refer to, they can only function by the operation of faith. So what does Paul specifically mean when He refers to this special manifestation of faith as a gift? The manifestation of the Spirit that is often termed the "gift of faith" would be more accurately called, simply, "faith." To begin with, this mention of faith must be understood in light of all the other things that are said about faith. The topic of faith is not only outlined in hundreds of verses, but faith is one of the primary subjects of scripture. It would be unwise to create a unique kind of faith from one verse of scripture. We must understand that faith touches every aspect of the spiritual.

Healings, miracles and revelatory speech were everyday occurrences in the Church. Therefore, in this case, Paul emphasizes a unique function of faith that may not have the same overt display of power as these other manifestations of the Spirit. However, great champions of faith testify that, through this activity of faith, God drops an impossible undertaking into our hearts and we know that we can accomplish it, or, similarly, He gives us the certainty that something has been done. The same thing happened to us when we were saved; we knew that all we had to do was respond and the miracle of salvation would take place. When the Holy Spirit ministers faith to us, then it becomes a word of faith in our mouth and a certainty of faith in our hearts that has no shadow of doubt. With this faith we have the assurance of salvation, and the same Spirit that assures us of salvation also speaks faith so that we can go and subdue a nation with the gospel of Jesus Christ. In this faith we find a special authority to do very specific things that the Holy Spirit gives us to do. It is certainty for a special work, not a different kind of faith. The ministry of the Spirit that speaks faith will take us far beyond all that we can think or ask. By the supply of the Spirit we are empowered to function in special works of grace and divine abilities. Therefore, we can understand that the faith that comes by hearing the word is the same faith that is supplied to us by the Holy Spirit.

The faith that began in our life when we were saved is meant to grow and mature. Faith grows and increases in our lives as we fellowship with God and do those things that He commands us to do.[165] Faith can grow to the place that one is full of faith; just like Steven was full of faith, who then because of that faith did great wonders and miracles. Faith can also remain dormant and not be activated in our lives because we fail to obey the Word of God and step out and do those things that He commands. We can confine and limit this faith through fear and self-reliance. If faith is to be activated in our lives, then we must step out as Abraham did and trust God. If we will turn our ears away from hearing the suggestions of the world around us and give ourselves wholly to walking in the Spirit, then a great flood of divine ability will be realized in our lives. The opportunity to live in a whole new world, a heavenly realm, is available to those who will walk by faith. We have received the same Spirit of faith and there is no reason to hesitate to speak the words of God, with confidence and boldness, in our everyday walk of life. We must give ourselves to the instructions and inspirations of the

Holy Spirit and be taught how to function in faith through the practical application of the Word of God. As we fellowship with Jesus in this walk of faith and obedience, faith will increase and the fullness of the faith of Jesus Christ will be seen in us.

Believing for the Impossible

Faith makes the impossible possible. "Jesus said to him if you are able to have faith nothing is impossible for the one who has faith" (Mark 9:23). There are too many people who think that great faith only belongs to the spiritually elite, but this is not true. God has made faith available to anyone who is willing. The father of the demon possessed boy that Jesus gave this opportunity to was of no importance. He was an ordinary, everyday person, yet Jesus revealed to him that he could take hold of a faith in which everything would become possible!

Faith calls forth the miraculous. It was faith that would make everything possible and enable an unknown man to be empowered to do anything. It was faith that made the woman with the issue of blood completely well.[166] When Jairus heard the news of the death of His daughter, Jesus demanded faith from him if he was going to see his daughter alive again.[167] It was the blind man's faith that caused him to regain his sight.[168]

We must understand that if we are going to realize all of the promises and blessings, then we must also have the faith that only comes by Jesus Christ. Jesus never looked at any faithless person and said "oh that's alright, not everyone has faith." Rather, when he saw people without faith He said, "Oh faithless and perverse generation how long must I be among you? How much longer must I put up with you (Mark 9:19)? He rebuked His disciples for not having it.[169] He didn't say, "oh guys it's alright, I know it takes time to develop faith;" rather, it is that which God expects to find in those who will walk with Him.

The absence of faith stands in the way of God and limits the miraculous expression of His love that would otherwise heal and deliver those bound and oppressed with sickness and disease.[170]

We can be certain that Christ Jesus demands faith from us today! If an unknown man in Israel can be expected to have faith that would empower him to do every impossible thing, how much more does God expect of us who have been both born of the Spirit and baptized in the Spirit? If the unbelief expressed in the town of Nazareth limited the power of Jesus, how much more will an unbelieving church hinder the works of grace! Every person must realize that faith only begins where human ability ends. We cannot say that we are waking in faith if we are living within the limits of human ability. We must be willing to step out and believe God for what only God can do. We must be willing to live like Jesus is in charge of everything, because He is. We must be willing to see that His authority is absolute and place our confidence in Him. We must allow the Spirit of truth to lead us into the truth where we believe that everything is possible to those who have faith.

The Spirit of Faith

"But we have the same Spirit of faith according to the scripture, I believed so I have spoke, we also believe and so we speak."

2 Corinthians 4:13

It is the Holy Spirit who is the supplier of faith, and this passage of scripture should be rightly understood as referring to that which proceeds from the Holy Spirit, and therefore, the "Spirit of faith" should be understood as a synonym for the Holy

Spirit.[171] Matthew Henry says in his commentary regarding this verse, "faith which is the operation of the Spirit;" therefore that which comes from the Holy Ghost and not from man. We have the same Spirit of faith that was given to Jesus, which is the same Spirit of faith that has operated in those in the past. The Spirit of faith will display great power and authority in those who will believe.

Paul, like the psalmist, is faced with death and affliction. However, because of the Spirit of faith, he, like the psalmist, was inspired to testify of the glory and power of God that rested upon him. Paul makes it clear that for the Word of God to work, it must be spoken: "for with the mouth confession is made unto salvation" (Romans 10:9-10). When Paul spoke the word of faith by the Spirit, he was doing so out of the treasure that was placed in his life.[172] There is a power at work on the inside of every believer, inspiring us to believe God – and that power is the Holy Spirit. It is out of this treasure of the new creation that the power of God brings forth His glory in us. Our spirit is joined unto the Spirit of the Lord, and as we yield to Him the things that He possesses are ours.

The Holy Spirit has placed the word of faith in our hearts and upon our lips so that we may declare the wonderful works of God. He has given us the authority of faith that calls those things that are not as though they were, and from such faith we inherit blessings and do the works of God. Through faith we become the beneficiaries of all the blessings that God has poured out upon His church.[173] The same Spirit of faith that prophesied through the psalmist of old was speaking through Paul, declaring to us that we have also been entrusted with the authority to speak and declare the promises of God.[174] Walk in the Spirit, and speak by the Spirit as the oracles of God. Let the word of Christ dwell in you, and speak those things that God believes. The Spirit of faith will arise within you and you will confidently proclaim that all of His promises are yes and amen! When the Spirit of faith speaks, the promises of God are received and the riches of God are revealed through our lives. [175]

The Word of Faith

"But what does it say, "The word is near you in your mouth and even in your heart;" this is that word of faith that is proclaimed."

Romans 10:8

God's people have the power that framed the universe within them. The Word of God will work mightily through you and accomplish great things if you will agree with God. All we must do is believe in our hearts and confess with our mouths those things that God has said, and then we will begin to participate with God's miracle. When Christ Jesus came into our hearts, the miracle power of the Living Word was established there. The Spirit of the Living God wrote His words of faith upon our hearts and minds. As we speak His words of faith by the Spirit, all of His will begins to take place through our lives. We made a confession of salvation and we believed in our hearts, and then the miracle of His life began in us and His righteousness was established. This is not only how we begin this miracle life with God, but it is also how we continue on in this walk of faith.

When we hear the Word of God, we are hearing the faith of God. This testimony of faith was first announced at Sinai. All of Israel audibly heard the words of the Almighty at the first Pentecost in the wilderness.[176] As the mountain shook with His presence, the Earth was filled with the sound of His voice declaring and revealing His word. They knew first-hand that God had spoken and not man.[177] All they needed to do was simply agree and all of the blessings that He had promised would have been theirs.

More than 2000 church leaders supported the crusade - Pastor Mark and his interpreter, Baal Shiva, ministering to pastors and leaders of the Nepali churches, with Pastor Anne Spitsbergen and Evangelist John Ward.

Today, the Word of God is present in our hearts and in our mouths (if we have been transformed by the word of His grace). [178] All we need to do is to speak out those things that the Word of God proclaimed and we will be speaking faith! As we speak faith, the blessings of Heaven described in the word will be revealed through our lives. It was the word of faith that created the vast expanse of the Universe, it was the word of faith that brought forth our salvation, and it is the word of faith that will cause us to possess all those wonderful things that God has promised.[179]

Too many of God's people speak things that have nothing to do with the Word of God and therefore nothing to do with faith —and whatsoever is not of faith is sin! They agree with disappointment and speak out a future of failure and demise. We must learn to speak only those things that God has said and not agree with our adversary or the disappointing circumstances that we may find ourselves facing. We live our lives much too earthly, so when things are going well we are happy, but when things go badly we are sad and begin to declare reproachful things that belong to the spirits of doubt and unbelief. God desires to turn all the bad around and fill you with a sound of continual thanksgiving. So, keep your tongue from evil and do not allow your lips to speak out words of doubt and disappointment, depart from evil and pursue His peace.[180] Only speak the truth, the word of faith, which God has spoken, and forever forsake the damnable heresy of murmur and complaint. God's word is forever settled in Heaven, so hold fast to what He has said. Say with the men of faith and wisdom, "All of the words of my mouth are in righteousness; there is nothing arrogant or perverse in them" (Proverbs 8:8).

The Authority of Faith from the Authority of the Word

God is a God of faith and without faith we cannot please Him. There is no good thing that He will withhold from those who walk uprightly. The upright life is found in believing the promises of God. So be in expectation that all that God has promised will be fulfilled in you.[181] Do not faint, nor grow weary.[182] Rather, let the words of your mouth and the meditations of your heart be acceptable in the sight of the One who is your Strength and Redeemer.[183] It is by our words that we are condemned and it is by our words that we are justified. Therefore, we must be careful to only speak the words of truth and the words of faith.[184] Our confession must be what God has said. Those who are born of the Spirit must learn to walk in the Spirit of truth as it is revealed by the Word of God, and not by anything else!

God makes faith easy for us to understand by giving us

models of faith like Abraham. Faith comes from a direct interaction and fellowship with God: He speaks and we believe and then obey! "As also it is written, 'I have made you a father of many nations – before God whom you have believed: who gives life to those that are dead, and calls into existence the things that do not exist'" (Romans 4:17). The foundation of faith is an absolute trust in God. Abraham trusted God, left the protection of his homeland and family and followed God even when he did not know where he was going.[185] Abraham stepped into a relationship with God, and that brought into his life a certainty that God's promises were true. Abraham was convinced that what God said, He would also do.[186] Abraham became the father, and an example, of faith to all who would follow after him. Even when everything was against him and it appeared that the promise had passed him by, he did not stagger at the promises of God, but remained strong in faith.[187]

Evangelist John Ward ministering the love and grace of the Lord Jesus Christ!

God makes operating in faith easy; all we need to do is rely upon the Holy Spirit. The Word of God declares to us what God has promised, and the Holy Spirit supplies us with the boldness and confidence that it will be done. The Spirit of truth speaks faith so that we can have all that God has promised. If we do not live in the realm of faith, then we are left to those things that only the arm of flesh can do.[188] To have the supply of faith that God has provided for us demands that we have a personal relationship with the Holy Spirit and yield ourselves to His influence. We need to recognize His place in our life and allow God to develop within us a dependency upon Him. Faith is not something that we can do on our own; it is something that we depend upon God to give us.

Faith enables us to see the results that God has promised, and causes us to rejoice as though it was already done! Childlike faith is all that is needed for God to do great works for us and through us. Men depend on their wisdom, insight, and maturity to accomplish things; God just wants us to trust Him and allow the Holy Spirit to fill us with the authority of mountain-moving faith!

The Word of God is the word of faith, and when we hear faith we are positioned to do the impossible. If we delay or refuse to step out, then the miracle will not come. Many listen to the word that produces faith, but for many different reasons do not do what God commands and find themselves left out. Our lives should only be about doing the will of the Father, and it is His word alone that describes what He has willed. There is no reason to be lost in the meaning of the Greek words, whether it is the 'logos' or the 'rhema,' because both may be used interchangeably. Besides, the written word immediately becomes the spoken word as soon as the preacher begins to speak.[189] When we hear the Word of God and obey, then faith is activated by the Spirit to produce God's divine results.

Pastors and leaders worshipping Jesus!

We are to walk by faith, and whatever is not of faith is sin! The walk of faith is lived out through obedience to the Word of God. The walk of faith that we must have is walking in the Spirit. The walk of faith is doing the will of the Father, and it is this life that we must live! The faith that comes by hearing what the Spirit of God speaks will always produce the results that the Word of God describes. When Peter heard the word of faith that Jesus spoke, he immediately began to do what he had never done before. He heard the word, and then stepped out and walked upon the water.

God is the Amen-God, and all of His promises are "Amen" as well.[190] God, who watches over His word to perform it, will perform it in you and me! Everywhere we go with God, there is faith for us to have. He is the God of faith, and without faith we cannot please Him. The Word of God is infused with faith, and the Holy Spirit activates it in the lives of all who will obey. The faith that He gives will come to us as we step out to do what He has spoken. The Holy Spirit is focused on faith in us; faith to see people saved, to walk in the gifts of the Spirit, to mature in the things of Christ and to advance the kingdom of God on the

Earth. Faith is looking for those who are sick, so that they may be healed, and those who are broken, so that they may be made whole. When we believe God's report, the report that He has spoken by the mouth of His servants, then we will see the hand of the Lord revealed in our lives.[191]

Pastors and leaders worshipping the Lord Jesus Christ!

The authority of the Word of God is all the authority that we need in order to step out and represent the kingdom. God has vested all divine power in His word, and if we will believe and give our lives to do what God commands, then the authority of faith will be revealed through us. We do not need to try to second-guess God, or look to some unique provision to have the faith that God demands, but simply do what the Bible says and speak what it has spoken; then the power of faith will go to work. Just as with Steven, who was full of faith and did great wonders and miracles among the people, faith will fill your hearts and mouths, and then the kingdom of the dear Son will be revealed through you. The Word of God will last forever, not one single part of it will fail; everything that Jesus has spoken will be fulfilled in those who will believe. Those who will hear the word and do what it says will have the life of faith! What price is there to pay, and what does God require? You must forsake your own way, your own thoughts and step into a realm where nothing is impossible for those who will believe!

Endnotes

[1] Matthew 12:28 But if I cast out devils by the Spirit of God, then the kingdom of God is come unto you; Luke 11:20 But if I with the finger of God cast out devils, no doubt the kingdom of God is come upon you.

[2] Matthew 4:23 And Jesus went about all Galilee, teaching in their synagogues, and preaching the gospel of the kingdom, and healing all manner of sickness and all manner of disease among the people; Mt 9:35 And Jesus went about all the cities and villages, teaching in their synagogues, and preaching the gospel of the kingdom, and healing every sickness and every disease among the people.*

[3] John 3:2 The same came to Jesus by night, and said unto him, Rabbi, we know that thou art a teacher come from God: for no man can do these miracles that thou doest, except God be with him.10:25 Jesus answered them, I told you, and ye believed not: the works that I do in my Father's name, they bear witness of me; 10:38 But if I do, though ye believe not me, believe the works: that ye may know, and believe, that the Father is in me, and I in him.

[4] Luke 7:22-23 Then Jesus answering said unto them, Go your way, and tell John what things ye have seen and heard; how that the blind see, the lame walk, the lepers are cleansed, the deaf hear, the dead are raised, to the poor the gospel is preached. And blessed is he, whosoever shall not be offended in me; John 14:12 Verily, verily, I say unto you, He that believeth on me, the works that I do shall he do also; and greater works than these shall he do; because I go unto my Father.

[5] Matthew 4:19 And he saith unto them, Follow me, and I will make you fishers of men; 8:22 But Jesus said unto him, Follow me; and let the dead bury their dead. 9:9 And as Jesus passed forth from thence, he saw a man, named Matthew, sitting at the receipt of custom: and he saith unto him, Follow me. And he arose, and followed him. Mark 8:34 And when he had called the people unto him with his disciples also, he said unto them,

Whosoever will come after me, let him deny himself, and take up his cross, and follow me.

[6] Mark 1:39 And he preached in their synagogues throughout all Galilee, and cast out devils; 3:15 And to have power to heal sicknesses, and to cast out devils; Matthew 9:32 As they went out, behold, they brought to him a dumb man possessed with a devil. 33 And when the devil was cast out, the dumb spake: and the multitudes marveled, saying, It was never so seen in Israel; 10:1 And when he had called unto him his twelve disciples, he gave them power against unclean spirits, to cast them out, and to heal all manner of sickness and all manner of disease.

[7] Luke 10:19 Behold, I give unto you power to tread on serpents and scorpions, and over all the power of the enemy: and nothing shall by any means hurt you. 1 John 4:4 Ye are of God, little children, and have overcome them: because greater is he that is in you, than he that is in the world; 5:18We know that whosoever is born of God sinneth not; but he that is begotten of God keepeth himself, and that wicked one toucheth him not.

[8] Matthew 10: 7 And as ye go, preach, saying, The kingdom of heaven is at hand. 8Heal the sick, cleanse the lepers, raise the dead, cast out devils: freely ye have received, freely give; Luke 9:2And he sent them to preach the kingdom of God, and to heal the sick.

[9] John 12:31 Now is the judgment of this world: now shall the prince of this world be cast out. 32 And I, if I be lifted up from the earth, will draw all men unto me; 16: 11 Of judgment, because the prince of this world is judged; 1 John 3:8 He that committeth sin is of the devil; for the devil sinneth from the beginning. For this purpose the Son of God was manifested, that he might destroy the works of the devil.

[10] Matthew 16:19 And I will give unto thee the keys of the kingdom of heaven: and whatsoever thou shalt bind on earth shall

be bound in heaven: and whatsoever thou shalt loose on earth shall be loosed in heaven; 18:18 Verily I say unto you, Whatsoever ye shall bind on earth shall be bound in heaven: and whatsoever ye shall loose on earth shall be loosed in heaven.

[11] John 14:1 12 Verily, verily, I say unto you, He that believeth on me, the works that I do shall he do also; and greater works than these shall he do; because I go unto my Father; Acts 2:39For the promise is unto you, and to your children, and to all that are afar off, even as many as the Lord our God shall call. Matthew 24:14 This gospel of the kingdom must be preached in all the world for a witness unto all nations, and then the end shall come

[12] Hebrews 2:14 Forasmuch then as the children are partakers of flesh and blood, he also himself likewise took part of the same; that through death he might destroy him that had the power of death, that is, the devil; 2 Timothy 1:10 But is now made manifest by the appearing of our Saviour Jesus Christ, who hath abolished death, and hath brought life and immortality to light through the gospel; Colossians 2:15 And having spoiled principalities and powers, he made a shew of them openly, triumphing over them in it.

[13] Ephesians 1:22-23 And hath put all things under his feet, and gave him to be the head over all things to the church, Which is his body, the fulness of him that filleth all in all; 2:6 And hath raised us up together, and made us sit together in heavenly places in Christ Jesus; Matthew 16:18And I say also unto thee, That thou art Peter, and upon this rock I will build my church; and the gates of hell shall not prevail against it.

[14] Ephesians 6:10 Finally, my brethren, be strong in the Lord, and in the power of his might; Matthew 28:18-19And Jesus came and spake unto them, saying, All power is given unto me in heaven and in earth. Go ye therefore, and teach all nations,

baptizing them in the name of the Father, and of the Son, and of the Holy Ghost:

[15] Ephesians 1:19-21 And what is the exceeding greatness of his power to us-ward who believe, according to the working of his mighty power, Which he wrought in Christ, when he raised him from the dead, and set him at his own right hand in the heavenly places, Far above all principality, and power, and might, and dominion, and every name that is named, not only in this world, but also in that which is to come:

[16] Acts 26:18a To open their eyes, and to turn them from darkness to light, and from the power of Satan unto God,

[17] Matthew 21:43 Therefore say I unto you, The kingdom of God shall be taken from you, and given to a nation bringing forth the fruits thereof; Romans 11: 23-24 And they also, if they abide not still in unbelief, shall be graffed in: for God is able to graff them in again. For if thou wert cut out of the olive tree which is wild by nature, and wert grafted contrary to nature into a good olive tree: how much more shall these, which be the natural branches, be graffed into their own olive tree?

[18] 1 Corinthians 12: 27 Now ye are the body of Christ, and members in particular; Ephesians 1:23 Which is his body, the fulness of him that filleth all in all; 5: 30 For we are members of his body, of his flesh, and of his bones; Col 1:18 And he is the head of the body, the church: who is the beginning, the firstborn from the dead; that in all things he might have the preeminence; John 1:16 And of his fulness have all we received, and grace for grace.

[19] Colossians 1:13 Who hath delivered us from the power of darkness, and hath translated us into the kingdom of his dear Son; 1 Th 2:12 That ye would walk worthy of God, who hath called you unto his kingdom and glory. John 17:22-23 And the glory which thou gavest me I have given them; that they may be one, even as we are one: I in them, and thou in me, that they may be made

perfect in one; and that the world may know that thou hast sent me, and hast loved them, as thou hast loved me. 1 John 3:24 And he that keepeth his commandments dwelleth in him, and he in him. And hereby we know that he abideth in us, by the Spirit which he hath given us. 2 Co 1:21 Now he which stablisheth us with you in Christ, and hath anointed us, is God;

[20] Mt 4:23 And Jesus went about all Galilee, teaching in their synagogues, and preaching the gospel of the kingdom, and healing all manner of sickness and all manner of disease among the people; Mark 1:14 Now after that John was put in prison, Jesus came into Galilee, preaching the gospel of the kingdom of God, Ac 20:25 And now, behold, I know that ye all, among whom I have gone preaching the kingdom of God, shall see my face no more; 1Corinthians 4:20 For the kingdom of God is not in word, but in power. 1 Corinthians 2:4 And my speech and my preaching was not with enticing words of man's wisdom, but in demonstration of the Spirit and of power: 1 Thessalonians 1:5 For our gospel came not unto you in word only, but also in power, and in the Holy Ghost, and in much assurance; as ye know what manner of men we were among you for your sake.

[21] John 14: 16-17 And I will pray the Father, and he shall give you another Comforter, that he may abide with you for ever; Even the Spirit of truth; whom the world cannot receive, because it seeth him not, neither knoweth him: but ye know him; for he dwelleth with you, and shall be in you; 26 But the Comforter, which is the Holy Ghost, whom the Father will send in my name, he shall teach you all things, and bring all things to your remembrance, whatsoever I have said unto you.; 15: 26 But when the Comforter is come, whom I will send unto you from the Father, even the Spirit of truth, which proceedeth from the Father, he shall testify of me; 16:7 Nevertheless I tell you the truth; It is expedient for you that I go away: for if I go not away, the Comforter will not come unto you; but if I depart, I will send him unto you; 13-15 Howbeit when he, the Spirit of truth, is come, he

will guide you into all truth: for he shall not speak of himself; but whatsoever he shall hear, that shall he speak: and he will shew you things to come. He shall glorify me: for he shall receive of mine, and shall shew it unto you. All things that the Father hath are mine: therefore said I, that he shall take of mine, and shall shew it unto you; 1 Corinthians 12:7-11: But the manifestation of the Spirit is given to every man to profit withal. For to one is given by the Spirit the word of wisdom; to another the word of knowledge by the same Spirit; To another faith by the same Spirit; to another the gifts of healing by the same Spirit; To another the working of miracles; to another prophecy; to another discerning of spirits; to another divers kinds of tongues; to another the interpretation of tongues: But all these worketh that one and the selfsame Spirit, dividing to every man severally as he will; Acts 1:2 Until the day in which he was taken up, after that he through the Holy Ghost had given commandments unto the apostles whom he had chosen:; 13:2 As they ministered to the Lord, and fasted, the Holy Ghost said, Separate me Barnabas and Saul for the work whereunto I have called them; 4 So they, being sent forth by the Holy Ghost, departed unto Seleucia; and from thence they sailed to Cyprus; 15:28 For it seemed good to the Holy Ghost, and to us, to lay upon you no greater burden than these necessary things; 16:6 Now when they had gone throughout Phrygia and the region of Galatia, and were forbidden of the Holy Ghost to preach the word in Asia; 28 Take heed therefore unto yourselves, and to all the flock, over the which the Holy Ghost hath made you overseers, to feed the church of God, which he hath purchased with his own blood.

[22] John 14:23 Jesus answered and said unto him, If a man love me, he will keep my words: and my Father will love him, and we will come unto him, and make our abode with him.; 17: 21-23 That they all may be one; as thou, Father, art in me, and I in thee, that they also may be one in us: that the world may believe that thou hast sent me. And the glory which thou gavest me I have given them; that they may be one, even as we are one: I in them,

and thou in me, that they may be made perfect in one; and that the world may know that thou hast sent me, and hast loved them, as thou hast loved me.; 1 John 3: 24 And he that keepeth his commandments dwelleth in him, and he in him. And hereby we know that he abideth in us, by the Spirit which he hath given us; 4:15 Whosoever shall confess that Jesus is the Son of God, God dwelleth in him, and he in God; 1 Corinthians 3:16 Know ye not that ye are the temple of God, and that the Spirit of God dwelleth in you; 6: 19 What? know ye not that your body is the temple of the Holy Ghost which is in you, which ye have of God, and ye are not your own?; 2 Corinthians 6:16 And what agreement hath the temple of God with idols? for ye are the temple of the living God; as God hath said, I will dwell in them, and walk in them; and I will be their God, and they shall be my people; 13:5 Examine yourselves, whether ye be in the faith; prove your own selves. Know ye not your own selves, how that Jesus Christ is in you, except ye be reprobates; 2 Timothy 1:14 That good thing which was committed unto thee keep by the Holy Ghost which dwelleth in us.).

[23] Acts 2:33 Therefore being by the right hand of God exalted, and having received of the Father the promise of the Holy Ghost, he hath shed forth this, which ye now see and hear.; John 7:39 But this spake he of the Spirit, which they that believe on him should receive: for the Holy Ghost was not yet given; because that Jesus was not yet glorified; 14: 26 But the Comforter, which is the Holy Ghost, whom the Father will send in my name, he shall teach you all things, and bring all things to your remembrance, whatsoever I have said unto you; 15:26 But when the Comforter is come, whom I will send unto you from the Father, even the Spirit of truth, which proceedeth from the Father, he shall testify of me:.*

[24] Acts 2:22 Ye men of Israel, hear these words; Jesus of Nazareth, a man approved of God among you by miracles and wonders and signs, which God did by him in the midst of you, as ye yourselves also know; 10:38 How God anointed Jesus of

Nazareth with the Holy Ghost and with power: who went about doing good, and healing all that were oppressed of the devil; for God was with him.; John 1:33 And I knew him not: but he that sent me to baptize with water, the same said unto me, Upon whom thou shalt see the Spirit descending, and remaining on him, the same is he which baptizeth with the Holy Ghost; 3:34 For he whom God hath sent speaketh the words of God: for God giveth not the Spirit by measure unto him; Luke 4:14 And Jesus returned in the power of the Spirit into Galilee: and there went out a fame of him through all the region round about; 18 The Spirit of the Lord is upon me, because he hath anointed me to preach the gospel to the poor; he hath sent me to heal the brokenhearted, to preach deliverance to the captives, and recovering of sight to the blind, to set at liberty them that are bruised.

[25] 1 John 2:6 He that saith he abideth in him ought himself also so to walk, even as he walked; 4:17 Herein is our love made perfect, that we may have boldness in the day of judgment: because as he is, so are we in this world. Romans 8:14 For as many as are led by the Spirit of God, they are the sons of God; 16 The Spirit itself beareth witness with our spirit, that we are the children of God.

[26] Acts 1:8 But ye shall receive power, after that the Holy Ghost is come upon you: and ye shall be witnesses unto me both in Jerusalem, and in all Judaea, and in Samaria, and unto the uttermost part of the earth.; Luke 24: 49 And, behold, I send the promise of my Father upon you: but tarry ye in the city of Jerusalem, until ye be endued with power from on high; Romans 15:19 Through mighty signs and wonders, by the power of the Spirit of God; so that from Jerusalem, and round about unto Illyricum, I have fully preached the gospel of Christ; Acts 4:33And with great power gave the apostles witness of the resurrection of the Lord Jesus: and great grace was upon them all.; 5:32 And we are his witnesses of these things; and so is also the Holy Ghost, whom God hath given to them that obey him.

[27] Acts 2:16-18 But this is that which was spoken by the prophet Joel; And it shall come to pass in the last days, saith God, I will pour out of my Spirit upon all flesh: and your sons and your daughters shall prophesy, and your young men shall see visions, and your old men shall dream dreams: And on my servants and on my handmaidens I will pour out in those days of my Spirit; and they shall prophesy; 2:38-39 Then Peter said unto them, Repent, and be baptized every one of you in the name of Jesus Christ for the remission of sins, and ye shall receive the gift of the Holy Ghost. For the promise is unto you, and to your children, and to all that are afar off, even as many as the Lord our God shall call. 11:16-17 Then remembered I the word of the Lord, how that he said, John indeed baptized with water; but ye shall be baptized with the Holy Ghost. Forasmuch then as God gave them the like gift as he did unto us, who believed on the Lord Jesus Christ; what was I, that I could withstand God?

[28] Matthew 3:11 I indeed baptize you with water unto repentance: but he that cometh after me is mightier than I, whose shoes I am not worthy to bear: he shall baptize you with the Holy Ghost, and with fire; Mark 1:8 I indeed have baptized you with water: but he shall baptize you with the Holy Ghost.; Luke 3:16 John answered, saying unto them all, I indeed baptize you with water; but one mightier than I cometh, the latchet of whose shoes I am not worthy to unloose: he shall baptize you with the Holy Ghost and with fire.

[29] Acts 1:5 For John truly baptized with water; but ye shall be baptized with the Holy Ghost not many days hence; 19:2-4 He said unto them, Have ye received the Holy Ghost since ye believed? And they said unto him, We have not so much as heard whether there be any Holy Ghost. And he said unto them, Unto what then were ye baptized? And they said, Unto John's baptism. Then said Paul, John verily baptized with the baptism of repentance, saying unto the people, that they should believe on him which should come after him, that is, on Christ Jesus.

[30] Acts 4:33 And with great power gave the apostles witness of the resurrection of the Lord Jesus: and great grace was upon them all; 6: 8 And Stephen, full of faith and power, did great wonders and miracles among the people; 19:11-12 And God wrought special miracles by the hands of Paul: So that from his body were brought unto the sick handkerchiefs or aprons, and the diseases departed from them, and the evil spirits went out of them; Romans 15: 19 Through mighty signs and wonders, by the power of the Spirit of God; so that from Jerusalem, and round about unto Illyricum, I have fully preached the gospel of Christ; Hebrews 2: 4 God also bearing them witness, both with signs and wonders, and with divers miracles, and gifts of the Holy Ghost, according to his own will? 1 Corinthians 12:7 But the manifestation of the Spirit is given to every man to profit withal; 28 And God hath set some in the church, first apostles, secondarily prophets, thirdly teachers, after that miracles, then gifts of healings, helps, governments, diversities of tongues.

[31] Matthew 20:23a And he saith unto them, Ye shall drink indeed of my cup, and be baptized with the baptism that I am baptized with; John 14:12 Verily, verily, I say unto you, He that believeth on me, the works that I do shall he do also; and greater works than these shall he do; because I go unto my Father; 20:21-22 Then said Jesus to them again, Peace be unto you: as my Father hath sent me, even so send I you. 22 And when he had said this, he breathed on them, and saith unto them, Receive ye the Holy Ghost.

[32] Philippians 2: 7 But made himself of no reputation, and took upon him the form of a servant, and was made in the likeness of men: And being found in fashion as a man, he humbled himself, and became obedient unto death, even the death of the cross.; 2Co 8:9 For ye know the grace of our Lord Jesus Christ, that, though he was rich, yet for your sakes he became poor, that ye through his poverty might be rich. Hebrews 5: 8 Though he were a Son, yet learned he obedience by the things which he

suffered; Heb 2:16* For verily he took not on him the nature of angels; but he took on him the seed of Abraham.; 2:9 But we see Jesus, who was made a little lower than the angels for the suffering of death, crowned with glory and honour; that he by the grace of God should taste death for every man; John 17:5* And now, O Father, glorify thou me with thine own self with the glory which I had with thee before the world was; Isa 7:15 Butter and honey shall he eat, that he may know to refuse the evil, and choose the good.

[33] Mark 1:10 And straightway coming up out of the water, he saw the heavens opened, and the Spirit like a dove descending upon him: And there came a voice from heaven, saying, Thou art my beloved Son, in whom I am well pleased; John 1:33 And I knew him not: but he that sent me to baptize with water, the same said unto me, Upon whom thou shalt see the Spirit descending, and remaining on him, the same is he which baptizeth with the Holy Ghost.

[34] John 5:20 For the Father loveth the Son, and sheweth him all things that himself doeth: and he will shew him greater works than these, that ye may marvel; 10:38; 14:10-11 Believest thou not that I am in the Father, and the Father in me? the words that I speak unto you I speak not of myself: but the Father that dwelleth in me, he doeth the works. But if I do, though ye believe not me, believe the works: that ye may know, and believe, that the Father is in me, and I in him. Believe me that I am in the Father, and the Father in me: or else believe me for the very works' sake; Colossians 2:9 For in him dwelleth all the fulness of the Godhead bodily.

[35] Romans 8:17 And if children, then heirs; heirs of God, and joint-heirs with Christ; if so be that we suffer with him, that we may be also glorified together; Galatians 4:7 Wherefore thou art no more a servant, but a son; and if a son, then an heir of God through Christ.

[36] *John 1:16 And of his fulness have all we received, and grace for grace; Colossians 2:10 And ye are complete in him, which is the head of all principality and power; Ephesians 4:13 Till we all come in the unity of the faith, and of the knowledge of the Son of God, unto a perfect man, unto the measure of the stature of the fulness of Christ:*

[37] *Ephesians 3:18-19 May be able to comprehend with all saints what is the breadth, and length, and depth, and height; And to know the love of Christ, which passeth knowledge, that ye might be filled with all the fulness of God.*

[38] *Ephesians 4:13-14 Till we all come in the unity of the faith, and of the knowledge of the Son of God, unto a perfect man, unto the measure of the stature of the fulness of Christ: That we henceforth be no more children, tossed to and fro, and carried about with every wind of doctrine, by the sleight of men, and cunning craftiness, whereby they lie in wait to deceive; 1 John 4: 17 Herein is our love made perfect, that we may have boldness in the day of judgment: because as he is, so are we in this world.*

[39] *Romans 6:15-19 What then? shall we sin, because we are not under the law, but under grace? God forbid. Know ye not, that to whom ye yield yourselves servants to obey, his servants ye are to whom ye obey; whether of sin unto death, or of obedience unto righteousness? But God be thanked, that ye were the servants of sin, but ye have obeyed from the heart that form of doctrine which was delivered you. Being then made free from sin, ye became the servants of righteousness. I speak after the manner of men because of the infirmity of your flesh: for as ye have yielded your members servants to uncleanness and to iniquity unto iniquity; even so now yield your members servants to righteousness unto holiness.*

[40] *1 Corinthians 2:16 For who hath known the mind of the Lord, that he may instruct him? But we have the mind of Christ; Galatians 4:6 And because ye are sons, God hath sent forth the Spirit of his Son into your hearts, crying, Abba, Father; Romans*

13:14 But put ye on the Lord Jesus Christ, and make not provision for the flesh, to fulfill the lusts thereof; Galatians 3:27 For as many of you as have been baptized into Christ have put on Christ.

[41] John 14:23 Jesus answered and said unto him, If a man love me, he will keep my words: and my Father will love him, and we will come unto him, and make our abode with him; 17:23 I in them, and thou in me, that they may be made perfect in one; and that the world may know that thou hast sent me, and hast loved them, as thou hast loved me; 1Jo 1:3 That which we have seen and heard declare we unto you, that ye also may have fellowship with us: and truly our fellowship is with the Father, and with his Son Jesus Christ; Col 2:2 That their hearts might be comforted, being knit together in love, and unto all riches of the full assurance of understanding, to the acknowledgement of the mystery of God, and of the Father, and of Christ.

[42] 1Corinthians 6:17 But he that is joined unto the Lord is one Spirit; John 3:6That which is born of the flesh is flesh; and that which is born of the Spirit is spirit.

[43] John 17:22-23 And the glory which thou gavest me I have given them; that they may be one, even as we are one: I in them, and thou in me, that they may be made perfect in one; and that the world may know that thou hast sent me, and hast loved them, as thou hast loved me.

[44] Colossians 1:13 Who hath delivered us from the power of darkness, and hath translated us into the kingdom of his dear Son; 2Co 5:20 Now then we are ambassadors for Christ, as though God did beseech you by us: we pray you in Christ's stead, be ye reconciled to God.

[45] Ephesians 5:18 And be not drunk with wine, wherein is excess; but be filled with the Spirit; 3:16 That he would grant you, according to the riches of his glory, to be strengthened with might by his Spirit in the inner man; Colossians 1:11 Strengthened with

all might, according to his glorious power, unto all patience and longsuffering with joyfulness;

[46] Romans 14:17 For the kingdom of God is not meat and drink; but righteousness, and peace, and joy in the Holy Ghost.

[47] Jude 1:20 But ye, beloved, building up yourselves on your most holy faith, praying in the Holy Ghost; 1Corinthians 14:4 He that speaketh in an unknown tongue edifieth himself; but he that prophesieth edifieth the church; 14:15 What is it then? I will pray with the spirit, and I will pray with the understanding also: I will sing with the spirit, and I will sing with the understanding also; Eph 6:18 Praying always with all prayer and supplication in the Spirit, and watching thereunto with all perseverance and supplication for all saints;

[48] Romans 15:19 Through mighty signs and wonders, by the power of the Spirit of God; so that from Jerusalem, and round about unto Illyricum, I have fully preached the gospel of Christ.

[49] Matthew 3:11 I indeed baptize you with water unto repentance: but he that cometh after me is mightier than I, whose shoes I am not worthy to bear: he shall baptize you with the Holy Ghost, and with fire; Mark 1:8 I indeed have baptized you with water: but he shall baptize you with the Holy Ghost.; Luke 3:16 John answered, saying unto them all, I indeed baptize you with water; but one mightier than I cometh, the latchet of whose shoes I am not worthy to unloose: he shall baptize you with the Holy Ghost and with fire; John 1:33 And I knew him not: but he that sent me to baptize with water, the same said unto me, Upon whom thou shalt see the Spirit descending, and remaining on him, the same is he which baptizeth with the Holy Ghost.; Acts 1:5 For John truly baptized with water; but ye shall be baptized with the Holy Ghost not many days hence; 2:4 And they were all filled with the Holy Ghost, and began to speak with other tongues, as the Spirit gave them utterance; 10:46 For they heard them speak with tongues, and magnify God. Then answered Peter; 11:16 Then

remembered I the word of the Lord, how that he said, John indeed baptized with water; but ye shall be baptized with the Holy Ghost;19:6 And when Paul had laid his hands upon them, the Holy Ghost came on them; and they spake with tongues, and prophesied; 1 Corinthians 14:2 For he that speaketh in an unknown tongue speaketh not unto men, but unto God: for no man understandeth him; howbeit in the spirit he speaketh mysteries; 15 What is it then? I will pray with the spirit, and I will pray with the understanding also: I will sing with the spirit, and I will sing with the understanding also; 18 I thank my God, I speak with tongues more than ye all; 39 Wherefore, brethren, covet to prophesy, and forbid not to speak with tongues.

[50] *John 7:38-39 He that believeth on me, as the scripture hath said, out of his belly shall flow rivers of living water. But this spake he of the Spirit, which they that believe on him should receive: for the Holy Ghost was not yet given; because that Jesus was not yet glorified; Acts 2:33 Therefore being by the right hand of God exalted, and having received of the Father the promise of the Holy Ghost, he hath shed forth this, which ye now see and hear; Ephesians 1:19-20 And what is the exceeding greatness of his power to us-ward who believe, according to the working of his mighty power, Which he wrought in Christ, when he raised him from the dead, and set him at his own right hand in the heavenly places,*

[51] *Acts 1:5 For John truly baptized with water; but ye shall be baptized with the Holy Ghost not many days hence.*

[52] *Acts 11:17 Forasmuch then as God gave them the like gift as he did unto us, who believed on the Lord Jesus Christ; what was I, that I could withstand God; 15:8 And God, which knoweth the hearts, bare them witness, giving them the Holy Ghost, even as he did unto us.*

[53] *Acts 19:4-6 Then said Paul, John verily baptized with the baptism of repentance, saying unto the people, that they should*

believe on him which should come after him, that is, on Christ Jesus. When they heard this, they were baptized in the name of the Lord Jesus. And when Paul had laid his hands upon them, the Holy Ghost came on them; and they spake with tongues, and prophesied.

[54] Salvation- Romans 5:15-17 5 But not as the offence, so also is the free gift. For if through the offence of one many be dead, much more the grace of God, and the gift by grace, which is by one man, Jesus Christ, hath abounded unto many. And not as it was by one that sinned, so is the gift: for the judgment was by one to condemnation, but the free gift is of many offences unto justification. For if by one man's offence death reigned by one; much more they which receive abundance of grace and of the gift of righteousness shall reign in life by one, Jesus Christ; 6:23 For the wages of sin is death; but the gift of God is eternal life through Jesus Christ our Lord; Ephesians 2:8 For by grace are ye saved through faith; and that not of yourselves: it is the gift of God. Holy Ghost- John 7:38-39 He that believeth on me, as the scripture hath said, out of his belly shall flow rivers of living water. But this spake he of the Spirit, which they that believe on him should receive: for the Holy Ghost was not yet given; because that Jesus was not yet glorified.); Luke 24:49 And, behold, I send the promise of my Father upon you: but tarry ye in the city of Jerusalem, until ye be endued with power from on high; Acts 1:8 But ye shall receive power, after that the Holy Ghost is come upon you: and ye shall be witnesses unto me both in Jerusalem, and in all Judaea, and in Samaria, and unto the uttermost part of the earth; 2:38 Then Peter said unto them, Repent, and be baptized every one of you in the name of Jesus Christ for the remission of sins, and ye shall receive the gift of the Holy Ghost.; 8:20 But Peter said unto him, Thy money perish with thee, because thou hast thought that the gift of God may be purchased with money; 10:45 And they of the circumcision which believed were astonished, as many as came with Peter, because that on the Gentiles also was poured out the gift of the Holy Ghost; 11:17 For as much then as God gave them*

the like gift as he did unto us, who believed on the Lord Jesus Christ; what was I, that I could withstand God; 2 Timothy 1:6 Wherefore I put thee in remembrance that thou stir up the gift of God, which is in thee by the putting on of my hands.

[55] John 16:7 Nevertheless I tell you the truth; It is expedient for you that I go away: for if I go not away, the Comforter will not come unto you; but if I depart, I will send him unto you; 12-15 I have yet many things to say unto you, but ye cannot bear them now. Howbeit when he, the Spirit of truth, is come, he will guide you into all truth: for he shall not speak of himself; but whatsoever he shall hear, that shall he speak: and he will shew you things to come. He shall glorify me: for he shall receive of mine, and shall shew it unto you. All things that the Father hath are mine: therefore said I, that he shall take of mine, and shall shew it unto you.

[56] 1 Corinthians 2:9-10 But as it is written, Eye hath not seen, nor ear heard, neither have entered into the heart of man, the things which God hath prepared for them that love him. But God hath revealed them unto us by his Spirit: for the Spirit searcheth all things, yea, the deep things of God.

[57] John 14:13-14 And whatsoever ye shall ask in my name, that will I do, that the Father may be glorified in the Son. If ye shall ask any thing in my name, I will do it; 15:7If ye abide in me, and my words abide in you, ye shall ask what ye will, and it shall be done unto you; 15:16 Ye have not chosen me, but I have chosen you, and ordained you, that ye should go and bring forth fruit, and that your fruit should remain: that whatsoever ye shall ask of the Father in my name, he may give it you. 1Jo 3:22 And whatsoever we ask, we receive of him, because we keep his commandments, and do those things that are pleasing in his sight.

[58] Psalms 119:89 For ever, O LORD, thy word is settled in heaven; Psalms 138:2 I will worship toward thy holy temple, and

praise thy name for thy lovingkindness and for thy truth: for thou hast magnified thy word above all thy name.

[59] Hebrews 11:3 Through faith we understand that the worlds were framed by the word of God, so that things which are seen were not made of things which do appear; Ps 33:6 By the word of the LORD were the heavens made; and all the host of them by the breath of his mouth; John 1:3 All things were made by him; and without him was not any thing made that was made. Eph 3:9 And to make all men see what is the fellowship of the mystery, which from the beginning of the world hath been hid in God, who created all things by Jesus Christ; Col 1:16 For by him were all things created, that are in heaven, and that are in earth, visible and invisible, whether they be thrones, or dominions, or principalities, or powers: all things were created by him, and for him; Heb 1:2 Hath in these last days spoken unto us by his Son, whom he hath appointed heir of all things, by whom also he made the worlds;

[60] 1 Peter 1:12 Unto whom it was revealed, that not unto themselves, but unto us they did minister the things, which are now reported unto you by them that have preached the gospel unto you with the Holy Ghost sent down from heaven; which things the angels desire to look into.

[61] Acts 20:32 And now, brethren, I commend you to God, and to the word of his grace, which is able to build you up, and to give you an inheritance among all them which are sanctified; 1Peter 2:2 As newborn babes, desire the sincere milk of the word, that ye may grow thereby.

[62] 1 Thessalonians 2:13 For this cause also thank we God without ceasing, because, when ye received the word of God which ye heard of us, ye received it not as the word of men, but as it is in truth, the word of God, which effectually worketh also in you that believe.

[63] 1 Peter 1:25 But the word of the Lord endureth for ever. And this is the word which by the gospel is preached unto you; 2Corinthians 1:20 For all the promises of God in him are yea, and in him Amen, unto the glory of God by us; Mt 24:35 Heaven and earth shall pass away, but my words shall not pass away.

[64] John 14:15 If ye love me, keep my commandments; 15:10 If ye keep my commandments, ye shall abide in my love; even as I have kept my Father's commandments, and abide in his love. 1Jo 2:3-4 And hereby we do know that we know him, if we keep his commandments. He that saith, I know him, and keepeth not his commandments, is a liar, and the truth is not in him; Luke 7:21 Not every one that saith unto me, Lord, Lord, shall enter into the kingdom of heaven; but he that doeth the will of my Father which is in heaven; Jas 1:22 But be ye doers of the word, and not hearers only, deceiving your own selves.

[65] Romans 4:17 As it is written, I have made thee a father of many nations,) before him whom he believed, even God, who quickeneth the dead, and calleth those things which be not as though they were.

[66] Romans 10:8 But what saith it? The word is nigh thee, even in thy mouth, and in thy heart: that is, the word of faith, which we preach.

[67] John 15:3 Now ye are clean through the word which I have spoken unto you; Eph 5:26 That he might sanctify and cleanse it with the washing of water by the word; John17:17 Sanctify them through thy truth: thy word is truth.

[68] Matthew 14:28 And Peter answered him and said, Lord, if it be thou, bid me come unto thee on the water.

[69] Ezekiel 36:26-27 A new heart also will I give you, and a new spirit will I put within you: and I will take away the stony heart out of your flesh, and I will give you an heart of flesh. And I

will put my spirit within you, and cause you to walk in my statutes, and ye shall keep my judgments, and do them.

[70] Acts 6:8 And Stephen, full of faith and power, did great wonders and miracles among the people; 1 Thessalonians 1:5 For our gospel came not unto you in word only, but also in power, and in the Holy Ghost, and in much assurance; as ye know what manner of men we were among you for your sake; 1 Corinthians 2:4-5 And my speech and my preaching was not with enticing words of man's wisdom, but in demonstration of the Spirit and of power: That your faith should not stand in the wisdom of men, but in the power of God.

[71] 1 Corinthians 3:3 For ye are yet carnal: for whereas there is among you envying, and strife, and divisions, are ye not carnal, and walk as men; 1Corinthians 2:14 But the natural man receiveth not the things of the Spirit of God: for they are foolishness unto him: neither can he know them, because they are spiritually discerned; Luke 24:45 Then opened he their understanding, that they might understand the scriptures.

[72] Hebrews 4:2 For unto us was the gospel preached, as well as unto them: but the word preached did not profit them, not being mixed with faith in them that heard it; Romans 10:17 So then faith cometh by hearing, and hearing by the word of God.

[73] Luke 4:32 And they were astonished at his doctrine: for his word was with power; 36 And they were all amazed, and spake among themselves, saying, What a word is this! for with authority and power he commandeth the unclean spirits, and they come out; Mark 1:26 And when the unclean spirit had torn him, and cried with a loud voice, he came out of him.

[74] 2 Corinthians 4:13 We having the same spirit of faith, according as it is written, I believed, and therefore have I spoken; we also believe, and therefore speak;.

[75] John 10:38 But if I do, though ye believe not me, believe the works: that ye may know, and believe, that the Father is in me, and I in him; 14:10 Believest thou not that I am in the Father, and the Father in me? the words that I speak unto you I speak not of myself: but the Father that dwelleth in me, he doeth the works.

[76] Romans 1:16 For I am not ashamed of the gospel of Christ: for it is the power of God unto salvation to every one that believeth; to the Jew first, and also to the Greek; 1 Corinthians 1:18 For the preaching of the cross is to them that perish foolishness; but unto us which are saved it is the power of God; 24 But unto them which are called, both Jews and Greeks, Christ the power of God, and the wisdom of God; 2:4-5 And my speech and my preaching was not with enticing words of man's wisdom, but in demonstration of the Spirit and of power: That your faith should not stand in the wisdom of men, but in the power of God. Matthew 7:29 For he taught them as one having authority, and not as the scribes.

[77] Acts 3:16 And his name through faith in his name hath made this man strong, whom ye see and know: yea, the faith which is by him hath given him this perfect soundness in the presence of you all; Matthew 18:20 For where two or three are gathered together in my name, there am I in the midst of them.

[78] John 2:11 This beginning of miracles did Jesus in Cana of Galilee, and manifested forth his glory; and his disciples believed on him; 23 Now when he was in Jerusalem at the passover, in the feast day, many believed in his name, when they saw the miracles which he did; 4:48 Then said Jesus unto him, Except ye see signs and wonders, ye will not believe; 7:31 And many of the people believed on him, and said, When Christ cometh, will he do more miracles than these which this man hath done.

[79] Matthew 12:28 But if I cast out devils by the Spirit of God, then the kingdom of God is come unto you; Luke 4:18 The Spirit of the Lord is upon me, because he hath anointed me to

preach the gospel to the poor; he hath sent me to heal the brokenhearted, to preach deliverance to the captives, and recovering of sight to the blind, to set at liberty them that are bruised; Acts 8:6-7 And the people with one accord gave heed unto those things which Philip spake, hearing and seeing the miracles which he did. For unclean spirits, crying with loud voice, came out of many that were possessed with them: and many taken with palsies, and that were lame, were healed; 19:11-12 And God wrought special miracles by the hands of Paul: So that from his body were brought unto the sick handkerchiefs or aprons, and the diseases departed from them, and the evil spirits went out of them; 2 Corinthians 4:3-4 But if our gospel be hid, it is hid to them that are lost: In whom the god of this world hath blinded the minds of them which believe not, lest the light of the glorious gospel of Christ, who is the image of God, should shine unto them.

[80] Hebrews 1:3 Who being the brightness of his glory, and the express image of his person, and upholding all things by the word of his power, when he had by himself purged our sins, sat down on the right hand of the Majesty on high; Mark 16:20 And they went forth, and preached every where, the Lord working with them, and confirming the word with signs following. Amen.

[81] 1 Peter 4:11 If any man speak, let him speak as the oracles of God; if any man minister, let him do it as of the ability which God giveth: that God in all things may be glorified through Jesus Christ, to whom be praise and dominion for ever and ever. Amen; Luke 4:36 And they were all amazed, and spake among themselves, saying, What a word is this! for with authority and power he commandeth the unclean spirits, and they come out.

[82] Ephesians 1:18-19 The eyes of your understanding being enlightened; that ye may know what is the hope of his calling, and what the riches of the glory of his inheritance in the saints, And what is the exceeding greatness of his power to us-ward who believe, according to the working of his mighty power,

[83] Acts 2:21 And it shall come to pass, that whosoever shall call on the name of the Lord shall be saved; 4:12 Neither is there salvation in any other: for there is none other name under heaven given among men, whereby we must be saved; Romans 10:13 For whosoever shall call upon the name of the Lord shall be saved.)

[84] Ephesians 4:24 And that ye put on the new man, which after God is created in righteousness and true holiness; Col 3:10 And have put on the new man, which is renewed in knowledge after the image of him that created him; 2Co 5:17 Therefore if any man be in Christ, he is a new creature: old things are passed away; behold, all things are become new.

[85] Ephesians 2:2-3 Wherein in time past ye walked according to the course of this world, according to the prince of the power of the air, the spirit that now worketh in the children of disobedience: Among whom also we all had our conversation in times past in the lusts of our flesh, fulfilling the desires of the flesh and of the mind; and were by nature the children of wrath, even as others; 2 Peter 1:4 Whereby are given unto us exceeding great and precious promises: that by these ye might be partakers of the divine nature, having escaped the corruption that is in the world through lust.; Titus 3:5 Not by works of righteousness which we have done, but according to his mercy he saved us, by the washing of regeneration, and renewing of the Holy Ghost.

[86] Philippians 2:9-10 Wherefore God also hath highly exalted him, and given him a name which is above every name: That at the name of Jesus every knee should bow, of things in heaven, and things in earth, and things under the earth.

[87] John 15:16 Ye have not chosen me, but I have chosen you, and ordained you, that ye should go and bring forth fruit, and that your fruit should remain: that whatsoever ye shall ask of the Father in my name, he may give it you; John 14:13-14 And whatsoever ye shall ask in my name, that will I do, that the Father may be glorified in the Son. If ye shall ask any thing in my name, I

will do it; 16:23-24 And in that day ye shall ask me nothing. Verily, verily, I say unto you, Whatsoever ye shall ask the Father in my name, he will give it you. Hitherto have ye asked nothing in my name: ask, and ye shall receive, that your joy may be full; 26 At that day ye shall ask in my name: and I say not unto you, that I will pray the Father for you:

[88] John 14:20 At that day ye shall know that I am in my Father, and ye in me, and I in you; 17:23 I in them, and thou in me, that they may be made perfect in one; and that the world may know that thou hast sent me, and hast loved them, as thou hast loved me.

[89] Acts 16:18 And this did she many days. But Paul, being grieved, turned and said to the spirit, I command thee in the name of Jesus Christ to come out of her. And he came out the same hour.

[90] Acts 28:3-5 And when Paul had gathered a bundle of sticks, and laid them on the fire, there came a viper out of the heat, and fastened on his hand. And when the barbarians saw the venomous beast hang on his hand, they said among themselves, No doubt this man is a murderer, whom, though he hath escaped the sea, yet vengeance suffereth not to live. And he shook off the beast into the fire, and felt no harm.

[91] 1 Corinthians 14:2 For he that speaketh in an unknown tongue speaketh not unto men, but unto God: for no man understandeth him; howbeit in the spirit he speaketh mysteries.

[92] 1 Corinthians 12:10 To another the working of miracles; to another prophecy; to another discerning of spirits; to another divers kinds of tongues; to another the interpretation of tongues; 14:15 What is it then? I will pray with the spirit, and I will pray with the understanding also: I will sing with the spirit, and I will sing with the understanding also; 18 I thank my God, I speak with tongues more than ye all; 21 In the law it is written, With men of

other tongues and other lips will I speak unto this people; and yet for all that will they not hear me, saith the Lord; 39 Wherefore, brethren, covet to prophesy, and forbid not to speak with tongues.

[93] Acts 2:39 For the promise is unto you, and to your children, and to all that are afar off, even as many as the Lord our God shall call; Hebrews 13:20 Now the God of peace, that brought again from the dead our Lord Jesus, that great shepherd of the sheep, through the blood of the everlasting covenant,

[94] 1 John 3:22 And whatsoever we ask, we receive of him, because we keep his commandments, and do those things that are pleasing in his sight.

[95] Revelation 1:5 And from Jesus Christ, who is the faithful witness, and the first begotten of the dead, and the prince of the kings of the earth. Unto him that loved us, and washed us from our sins in his own blood; Ephesians 1:7In whom we have redemption through his blood, the forgiveness of sins, according to the riches of his grace; Romans 5:9 Much more then, being now justified by his blood, we shall be saved from wrath through him; Zechariah 13:1 In that day there shall be a fountain opened to the house of David and to the inhabitants of Jerusalem for sin and for uncleanness; Acts 20:28 Take heed therefore unto yourselves, and to all the flock, over the which the Holy Ghost hath made you overseers, to feed the church of God, which he hath purchased with his own blood.; Hebrews 9:14 How much more shall the blood of Christ, who through the eternal Spirit offered himself without spot to God, purge your conscience from dead works to serve the living God; 1 Peter 1:18-19 Forasmuch as ye know that ye were not redeemed with corruptible things, as silver and gold, from your vain conversation received by tradition from your fathers; But with the precious blood of Christ, as of a lamb without blemish and without spot:; 1 John 1:7 But if we walk in the light, as he is in the light, we have fellowship one with another, and the blood of Jesus Christ his Son cleanseth us from all sin.

[96] *1 Corinthians 6:20 For ye are bought with a price: therefore glorify God in your body, and in your spirit, which are God's; 7:23 Ye are bought with a price; be not ye the servants of men; Ephesians 1:13-14 In whom ye also trusted, after that ye heard the word of truth, the gospel of your salvation: in whom also after that ye believed, ye were sealed with that holy Spirit of promise, Which is the earnest of our inheritance until the redemption of the purchased possession, unto the praise of his glory.*

[97] *Colossians 2:15 And having spoiled principalities and powers, he made a shew of them openly, triumphing over them in it; Hebrews 2:14 Forasmuch then as the children are partakers of flesh and blood, he also himself likewise took part of the same; that through death he might destroy him that had the power of death, that is, the devil; 2 Timothy 1:10 But is now made manifest by the appearing of our Saviour Jesus Christ, who hath abolished death, and hath brought life and immortality to light through the gospel; John 12:31 Now is the judgment of this world: now shall the prince of this world be cast out; 16:11 Of judgment, because the prince of this world is judged.*

[98] *Psalm 103:3 Who forgiveth all thine iniquities; who healeth all thy diseases; Isaiah 53:5 He is despised and rejected of men; a man of sorrows, and acquainted with grief: and we hid as it were our faces from him; he was despised, and we esteemed him not; 1 Peter 2:24 Who his own self bare our sins in his own body on the tree, that we, being dead to sins, should live unto righteousness: by whose stripes ye were healed.; Matthew 8:16-17 When the even was come, they brought unto him many that were possessed with devils: and he cast out the spirits with his word, and healed all that were sick: That it might be fulfilled which was spoken by Esaias the prophet, saying, Himself took our infirmities, and bare our sicknesses; 9:6 But that ye may know that the Son of man hath power on earth to forgive sins, (then saith he to the sick of the palsy,) Arise, take up thy bed, and go unto thine house;*

12:15-18 But when Jesus knew it, he withdrew himself from thence: and great multitudes followed him, and he healed them all; And charged them that they should not make him known: That it might be fulfilled which was spoken by Esaias the prophet, saying, Behold my servant, whom I have chosen; my beloved, in whom my soul is well pleased: I will put my spirit upon him, and he shall shew judgment to the Gentiles.

[99] Titus 2:14 Who gave himself for us, that he might redeem us from all iniquity, and purify unto himself a peculiar people, zealous of good works; 1 Peter 1:22 Seeing ye have purified your souls in obeying the truth through the Spirit unto unfeigned love of the brethren, see that ye love one another with a pure heart fervently; Ephesians 5:27 That he might present it to himself a glorious church, not having spot, or wrinkle, or any such thing; but that it should be holy and without blemish; 1 John 1:9 If we confess our sins, he is faithful and just to forgive us our sins, and to cleanse us from all unrighteousness;1 Thessalonians 5:23 And the very God of peace sanctify you wholly; and I pray God your whole spirit and soul and body be preserved blameless unto the coming of our Lord Jesus Christ; 2 Peter 1:9 But he that lacketh these things is blind, and cannot see afar off, and hath forgotten that he was purged from his old sins; 3:14 Wherefore, beloved, seeing that ye look for such things, be diligent that ye may be found of him in peace, without spot, and blameless; 9:22 And almost all things are by the law purged with blood; and without shedding of blood is no remission; 10:10 By the which will we are sanctified through the offering of the body of Jesus Christ once for all; 14 For by one offering he hath perfected for ever them that are sanctified; 22 Let us draw near with a true heart in full assurance of faith, having our hearts sprinkled from an evil conscience, and our bodies washed with pure water; Philippians 2:15 That ye may be blameless and harmless, the sons of God, without rebuke, in the midst of a crooked and perverse nation, among whom ye shine as lights in the world.

[100] Matthew 26:28 For this is my blood of the new testament, which is shed for many for the remission of sins; Colossians 1:14 In whom we have redemption through his blood, even the forgiveness of sins; 1 John 2:1-2 My little children, these things write I unto you, that ye sin not. And if any man sin, we have an advocate with the Father, Jesus Christ the righteous: And he is the propitiation for our sins: and not for ours only, but also for the sins of the whole world; Romans 6:6 Knowing this, that our old man is crucified with him, that the body of sin might be destroyed, that henceforth we should not serve sin; 8:2 For the law of the Spirit of life in Christ Jesus hath made me free from the law of sin and death.

[101] Colossians 1:22 In the body of his flesh through death, to present you holy and unblameable and unreproveable in his sight; Romans 8:1 There is therefore now no condemnation to them which are in Christ Jesus, who walk not after the flesh, but after the Spirit.

[102] Romans 8:34 Who is he that condemneth? It is Christ that died, yea rather, that is risen again, who is even at the right hand of God, who also maketh intercession for us; Hebrews 7:25 Wherefore he is able also to save them to the uttermost that come unto God by him, seeing he ever liveth to make intercession for them; 1 Timothy 2:5 For there is one God, and one mediator between God and men, the man Christ Jesus; Hebrews 8:6 But now hath he obtained a more excellent ministry, by how much also he is the mediator of a better covenant, which was established upon better promises; 9:15 And for this cause he is the mediator of the new testament, that by means of death, for the redemption of the transgressions that were under the first testament, they which are called might receive the promise of eternal inheritance; 12:24 And to Jesus the mediator of the new covenant, and to the blood of sprinkling, that speaketh better things than that of Abel.

[103] Romans 3:26 *To declare, I say, at this time his righteousness: that he might be just, and the justifier of him which believeth in Jesus; Acts 13:38-39 Be it known unto you therefore, men and brethren, that through this man is preached unto you the forgiveness of sins: And by him all that believe are justified from all things, from which ye could not be justified by the law of Moses.*

[104] Acts 10:28 *And he said unto them, Ye know how that it is an unlawful thing for a man that is a Jew to keep company, or come unto one of another nation; but God hath shewed me that I should not call any man common or unclean; Ac 11:8 But I said, Not so, Lord: for nothing common or unclean hath at any time entered into my mouth; Ro 14:14 I know, and am persuaded by the Lord Jesus, that there is nothing unclean of itself: but to him that esteemeth any thing to be unclean, to him it is unclean.*

[105] Isaiah 1:18 *Come now, and let us reason together, saith the LORD: though your sins be as scarlet, they shall be as white as snow; though they be red like crimson, they shall be as wool.*

[106] Romans 8:2 *For the law of the Spirit of life in Christ Jesus hath made me free from the law of sin and death.*

[107] 1 Corinthians 5:7 *Purge out therefore the old leaven, that ye may be a new lump, as ye are unleavened. For even Christ our passover is sacrificed for us; John 13:1 Now before the feast of the passover, when Jesus knew that his hour was come that he should depart out of this world unto the Father, having loved his own which were in the world, he loved them unto the end; 19:4 Pilate therefore went forth again, and saith unto them, Behold, I bring him forth to you, that ye may know that I find no fault in him; 14-15 And it was the preparation of the passover, and about the sixth hour: and he saith unto the Jews, Behold your King! But they cried out, Away with him, away with him, crucify him. Pilate saith unto them, Shall I crucify your King? The chief priests answered, We have no king but Caesar.*

[108] Leviticus 16:5-22 And he shall take of the congregation of the children of Israel two kids of the goats for a sin offering, and one ram for a burnt offering. And Aaron shall offer his bullock of the sin offering, which is for himself, and make an atonement for himself, and for his house…

[109] Acts 5:31 Him hath God exalted with his right hand to be a Prince and a Saviour, for to give repentance to Israel, and forgiveness of sins.

[110] Hebrews 13:10 We have an altar, whereof they have no right to eat which serve the tabernacle.

[111] Ephesians 2:16 And that he might reconcile both unto God in one body by the cross, having slain the enmity thereby:

[112] John 12:32 And I, if I be lifted up from the earth, will draw all men unto me.

[113] Hebrews 10:19-20 Having therefore, brethren, boldness to enter into the holiest by the blood of Jesus, By a new and living way, which he hath consecrated for us, through the veil, that is to say, his flesh; Luke 23:45 And the sun was darkened, and the veil of the temple was rent in the midst.

[114] Isaiah 53:10 Yet it pleased the LORD to bruise him; he hath put him to grief: when thou shalt make his soul an offering for sin, he shall see his seed, he shall prolong his days, and the pleasure of the LORD shall prosper in his hand.

[115] Romans 8:32 He that spared not his own Son, but delivered him up for us all, how shall he not with him also freely give us all things?

[116] Galatians 2:20 I am crucified with Christ: nevertheless I live; yet not I, but Christ liveth in me: and the life which I now live in the flesh I live by the faith of the Son of God, who loved me, and gave himself for me.

[117] 2 Corinthians 5:14-15 For the love of Christ constraineth us; because we thus judge, that if one died for all, then were all dead: And that he died for all, that they which live should not henceforth live unto themselves, but unto him which died for them, and rose again; Romans 6:3-4 Know ye not, that so many of us as were baptized into Jesus Christ were baptized into his death? Therefore we are buried with him by baptism into death: that like as Christ was raised up from the dead by the glory of the Father, even so we also should walk in newness of life; 12:2 And be not conformed to this world: but be ye transformed by the renewing of your mind, that ye may prove what is that good, and acceptable, and perfect, will of God.

[118] Matthew 18:21-22 Then came Peter to him, and said, Lord, how oft shall my brother sin against me, and I forgive him? till seven times? Jesus saith unto him, I say not unto thee, Until seven times: but, Until seventy times seven.

[119] Hebrews 9:16 For where a testament is, there must also of necessity be the death of the testator.

[120] Romans 3:25 Whom God hath set forth to be a propitiation through faith in his blood, to declare his righteousness for the remission of sins that are past, through the forbearance of God;

[121] Colossians 1:22 In the body of his flesh through death, to present you holy and unblameable and unreproveable in his sight:

[122] 18:35 So likewise shall my heavenly Father do also unto you, if ye from your hearts forgive not every one his brother their trespasses.

[123] 1 Peter 1:2 Elect according to the foreknowledge of God the Father, through sanctification of the Spirit, unto obedience and sprinkling of the blood of Jesus Christ: Grace unto you, and peace, be multiplied; Hebrews 10:22 Let us draw near with a true heart

in full assurance of faith, having our hearts sprinkled from an evil conscience, and our bodies washed with pure water; Exodus 24:8 And Moses took the blood, and sprinkled it on the people, and said, Behold the blood of the covenant, which the LORD hath made with you concerning all these words; Hebrews 9:19 For when Moses had spoken every precept to all the people according to the law, he took the blood of calves and of goats, with water, and scarlet wool, and hyssop, and sprinkled both the book, and all the people.

[124] John 6:56-57 He that eateth my flesh, and drinketh my blood, dwelleth in me, and I in him. As the living Father hath sent me, and I live by the Father: so he that eateth me, even he shall live by me.

[125] 1 Corinthians 5:7 Purge out therefore the old leaven, that ye may be a new lump, as ye are unleavened. For even Christ our passover is sacrificed for us; Exodus 12:7 And they shall take of the blood, and strike it on the two side posts and on the upper door post of the houses, wherein they shall eat it.

[126] Matthew 26:26-28 And as they were eating, Jesus took bread, and blessed it, and brake it, and gave it to the disciples, and said, Take, eat; this is my body. And he took the cup, and gave thanks, and gave it to them, saying, Drink ye all of it; For this is my blood of the new testament, which is shed for many for the remission of sins.; 1 Corinthians 11:24-25 And when he had given thanks, he brake it, and said, Take, eat: this is my body, which is broken for you: this do in remembrance of me. After the same manner also he took the cup, when he had supped, saying, This cup is the new testament in my blood: this do ye, as oft as ye drink it, in remembrance of me.

[127] 1 Corinthians 11:26 For as often as ye eat this bread, and drink this cup, ye do shew the Lord's death till he come.

[128] John 15:4-5 Abide in me, and I in you. As the branch cannot bear fruit of itself, except it abide in the vine; no more can ye, except ye abide in me. I am the vine, ye are the branches: He that abideth in me, and I in him, the same bringeth forth much fruit: for without me ye can do nothing.

[129] John 6:53 Then Jesus said unto them, Verily, verily, I say unto you, Except ye eat the flesh of the Son of man, and drink his blood, ye have no life in you.

[130] Exodus 12:13 And the blood shall be to you for a token upon the houses where ye are: and when I see the blood, I will pass over you, and the plague shall not be upon you to destroy you, when I smite the land of Egypt.

[131] Numbers 16:46-48 And Moses said unto Aaron, Take a censer, and put fire therein from off the altar, and put on incense, and go quickly unto the congregation, and make an atonement for them: for there is wrath gone out from the LORD; the plague is begun. And Aaron took as Moses commanded, and ran into the midst of the congregation; and, behold, the plague was begun among the people: and he put on incense, and made an atonement for the people. And he stood between the dead and the living; and the plague was stayed.

[132] Hebrews 9:19 For when Moses had spoken every precept to all the people according to the law, he took the blood of calves and of goats, with water, and scarlet wool, and hyssop, and sprinkled both the book, and all the people; 10:22 Let us draw near with a true heart in full assurance of faith, having our hearts sprinkled from an evil conscience, and our bodies washed with pure water; 12:24 And to Jesus the mediator of the new covenant, and to the blood of sprinkling, that speaketh better things than that of Abel.

[133] Hebrews 2:17 Wherefore in all things it behoved him to be made like unto his brethren, that he might be a merciful and

faithful high priest in things pertaining to God, to make reconciliation for the sins of the people; 3:1 Wherefore, holy brethren, partakers of the heavenly calling, consider the Apostle and High Priest of our profession, Christ Jesus; 4:14 Seeing then that we have a great high priest, that is passed into the heavens, Jesus the Son of God, let us hold fast our profession; Matthew 26:28 For this is my blood of the new testament, which is shed for many for the remission of sins.

[134] *1 Peter 2:5 Ye also, as lively stones, are built up a spiritual house, an holy priesthood, to offer up spiritual sacrifices, acceptable to God by Jesus Christ; 9 But ye are a chosen generation, a royal priesthood, an holy nation, a peculiar people; that ye should shew forth the praises of him who hath called you out of darkness into his marvellous light:*

[135] *John 1:12 But as many as received him, to them gave he power to become the sons of God, even to them that believe on his name; 1 John 3:1-2 Behold, what manner of love the Father hath bestowed upon us, that we should be called the sons of God: therefore the world knoweth us not, because it knew him not. Beloved, now are we the sons of God, and it doth not yet appear what we shall be: but we know that, when he shall appear, we shall be like him; for we shall see him as he is.*

[136] *Galatians 4:6 And because ye are sons, God hath sent forth the Spirit of his Son into your hearts, crying, Abba, Father; Romans 8:15 For ye have not received the spirit of bondage again to fear; but ye have received the Spirit of adoption, whereby we cry, Abba, Father.*

[137] *Galatians 4:7 Wherefore thou art no more a servant, but a son; and if a son, then an heir of God through Christ.; Romans 8:17 And if children, then heirs; heirs of God, and joint-heirs with Christ; if so be that we suffer with him, that we may be also glorified together.*

[138] John 15:7 If ye abide in me, and my words abide in you, ye shall ask what ye will, and it shall be done unto you; 1 John 5:14 And this is the confidence that we have in him, that, if we ask any thing according to his will, he heareth us:

[139] John 1:16 And of his fulness have all we received, and grace for grace; Colossians 1:27 To whom God would make known what is the riches of the glory of this mystery among the Gentiles; which is Christ in you, the hope of glory; 2:9-10 For in him dwelleth all the fulness of the Godhead bodily. And ye are complete in him, which is the head of all principality and power.

[140] John 17:14 I have given them thy word; and the world hath hated them, because they are not of the world, even as I am not of the world; 16 They are not of the world, even as I am not of the world; Ephesians 1:9 Having made known unto us the mystery of his will, according to his good pleasure which he hath purposed in himself; 1 John 4:17 Herein is our love made perfect, that we may have boldness in the day of judgment: because as he is, so are we in this world.).

[141] 1 John 5:10-11 He that believeth on the Son of God hath the witness in himself: he that believeth not God hath made him a liar; because he believeth not the record that God gave of his Son. And this is the record, that God hath given to us eternal life, and this life is in his Son.

[142] Galatians 2:20 I am crucified with Christ: nevertheless I live; yet not I, but Christ liveth in me: and the life which I now live in the flesh I live by the faith of the Son of God, who loved me, and gave himself for me.; 3:27 For as many of you as have been baptized into Christ have put on Christ; Ro 6:4 Therefore we are buried with him by baptism into death: that like as Christ was raised up from the dead by the glory of the Father, even so we also should walk in newness of life; Col 2:12 Buried with him in baptism, wherein also ye are risen with him through the faith of the operation of God, who hath raised him from the dead..

[143] Galatians 1:16 To reveal his Son in me, that I might preach him among the heathen; immediately I conferred not with flesh and blood.

[144] Romans 8:29 For whom he did foreknow, he also did predestinate to be conformed to the image of his Son, that he might be the firstborn among many brethren.

[145] John 17:23 I in them, and thou in me, that they may be made perfect in one; and that the world may know that thou hast sent me, and hast loved them, as thou hast loved me.

[146] Philippians 3:14 I press toward the mark for the prize of the high calling of God in Christ Jesus; 21 Who shall change our vile body, that it may be fashioned like unto his glorious body, according to the working whereby he is able even to subdue all things unto himself; 1 Corinthians 15:49 And as we have borne the image of the earthy, we shall also bear the image of the heavenly; Ephesians 1: Which is the earnest of our inheritance until the redemption of the purchased possession, unto the praise of his glory.

[147] 2 Corinthians 5:1 For we know that if our earthly house of this tabernacle were dissolved, we have a building of God, an house not made with hands, eternal in the heavens.

[148] Romans 8:14-15 For as many as are led by the Spirit of God, they are the sons of God. 15 For ye have not received the spirit of bondage again to fear; but ye have received the Spirit of adoption, whereby we cry, Abba, Father; Galatians 4:6 And because ye are sons, God hath sent forth the Spirit of his Son into your hearts, crying, Abba, Father.*

[149] 1 Peter 2:21-23 For even hereunto were ye called: because Christ also suffered for us, leaving us an example, that ye should follow his steps: Who did no sin, neither was guile found in his mouth: Who, when he was reviled, reviled not again; when he

suffered, he threatened not; but committed himself to him that judgeth righteously; Philippians 1:21 For to me to live is Christ, and to die is gain; 2 Corinthians 5:14-15 For the love of Christ constraineth us; because we thus judge, that if one died for all, then were all dead: And that he died for all, that they which live should not henceforth live unto themselves, but unto him which died for them, and rose again.

[150] Ephesians 5:1 Be ye therefore followers of God, as dear children; Romans 8:29 For whom he did foreknow, he also did predestinate to be conformed to the image of his Son, that he might be the firstborn among many brethren.

[151] 2 Peter 3:13 Nevertheless we, according to his promise, look for new heavens and a new earth, wherein dwelleth righteousness; Isaiah 65:17 For, behold, I create new heavens and a new earth: and the former shall not be remembered, nor come into mind; 66:22 For as the new heavens and the new earth, which I will make, shall remain before me, saith the LORD, so shall your seed and your name remain; Revelation 21:1 And I saw a new heaven and a new earth: for the first heaven and the first earth were passed away; and there was no more sea.).

[152]Isaiah 35:10 And the ransomed of the LORD shall return, and come to Zion with songs and everlasting joy upon their heads: they shall obtain joy and gladness, and sorrow and sighing shall flee away; 51:11 Therefore the redeemed of the LORD shall return, and come with singing unto Zion; and everlasting joy shall be upon their head: they shall obtain gladness and joy; and sorrow and mourning shall flee away.

[153] Matthew 8:10 When Jesus heard it, he marvelled, and said to them that followed, Verily I say unto you, I have not found so great faith, no, not in Israel; 15:28 Then Jesus answered and said unto her, O woman, great is thy faith: be it unto thee even as thou wilt. And her daughter was made whole from that very hour; 17:20 And Jesus said unto them, Because of your unbelief: for

verily I say unto you, If ye have faith as a grain of mustard seed, ye shall say unto this mountain, Remove hence to yonder place; and it shall remove; and nothing shall be impossible unto you.; Mark 9:23 Jesus said unto him, If thou canst believe, all things are possible to him that believeth.

[154] Matthew 8:26-27 And he saith unto them, Why are ye fearful, O ye of little faith? Then he arose, and rebuked the winds and the sea; and there was a great calm. But the men marvelled, saying, What manner of man is this, that even the winds and the sea obey him!

[155] Hebrews 11:1-35).

[156] Romans 10:8-10 But what saith it? The word is nigh thee, even in thy mouth, and in thy heart: that is, the word of faith, which we preach; That if thou shalt confess with thy mouth the Lord Jesus, and shalt believe in thine heart that God hath raised him from the dead, thou shalt be saved. For with the heart man believeth unto righteousness; and with the mouth confession is made unto salvation..

[157] Galatians 2:20 I am crucified with Christ: nevertheless I live; yet not I, but Christ liveth in me: and the life which I now live in the flesh I live by the faith of the Son of God, who loved me, and gave himself for me.; Romans 6:4 Therefore we are buried with him by baptism into death: that like as Christ was raised up from the dead by the glory of the Father, even so we also should walk in newness of life; Ephesians 2:5-6 Even when we were dead in sins, hath quickened us together with Christ, (by grace ye are saved;) 6 And hath raised us up together, and made us sit together in heavenly places in Christ Jesus; Colossians 3:1-4 If ye then be risen with Christ, seek those things which are above, where Christ sitteth on the right hand of God. Set your affection on things above, not on things on the earth. For ye are dead, and your life is hid with Christ in God. When Christ, who is our life, shall appear, then shall ye also appear with him in glory.*

[158] 2 Corinthians 13:5 Examine yourselves, whether ye be in the faith; prove your own selves. Know ye not your own selves, how that Jesus Christ is in you, except ye be reprobates; John 15:1-5 I am the true vine, and my Father is the husbandman. Every branch in me that beareth not fruit he taketh away: and every branch that beareth fruit, he purgeth it, that it may bring forth more fruit. Now ye are clean through the word which I have spoken unto you. Abide in me, and I in you. As the branch cannot bear fruit of itself, except it abide in the vine; no more can ye, except ye abide in me. I am the vine, ye are the branches: He that abideth in me, and I in him, the same bringeth forth much fruit: for without me ye can do nothing.

[159] 2 Corinthians 4:13 We having the same spirit of faith, according as it is written, I believed, and therefore have I spoken; we also believe, and therefore speak; Acts 3:16 And his name through faith in his name hath made this man strong, whom ye see and know: yea, the faith which is by him hath given him this perfect soundness in the presence of you all.

[160] Mark 11:24 Therefore I say unto you, What things soever ye desire, when ye pray, believe that ye receive them, and ye shall have them; 1 John 5:14-15 And this is the confidence that we have in him, that, if we ask any thing according to his will, he heareth us: And if we know that he hear us, whatsoever we ask, we know that we have the petitions that we desired of him; Acts 10:43 To him give all the prophets witness, that through his name whosoever believeth in him shall receive remission of sins; Galatians 3:2 This only would I learn of you, Received ye the Spirit by the works of the law, or by the hearing of faith; Romans 4:17 As it is written, I have made thee a father of many nations, before him whom he believed, even God, who quickeneth the dead, and calleth those things which be not as though they were; Romans 4:20-21 He staggered not at the promise of God through unbelief; but was strong in faith, giving glory to God; And being fully persuaded that, what he had promised, he was able also to

perform; 2 Corinthians 1:20 For all the promises of God in him are yea, and in him Amen, unto the glory of God by us.

[161] Mark 11:22 And Jesus answering saith unto them, Have faith in God; Galatians 5:22 But the fruit of the Spirit is love, joy, peace, longsuffering, gentleness, goodness, faith; Jude 1:20 But ye, beloved, building up yourselves on your most holy faith, praying in the Holy Ghost; 1 Corinthians 14:9 So likewise ye, except ye utter by the tongue words easy to be understood, how shall it be known what is spoken? for ye shall speak into the air.

[162] Galatians 3:2 This only would I learn of you, Received ye the Spirit by the works of the law, or by the hearing of faith?; 6 Even as Abraham believed God, and it was accounted to him for righteousness.

[163] Galatians 3:3 Are ye so foolish? having begun in the Spirit, are ye now made perfect by the flesh?

[164] 1 Corinthians 12:9 To another faith by the same Spirit; to another the gifts of healing by the same Spirit;

[165] 2 Thessalonians 1:3 We are bound to thank God always for you, brethren, as it is meet, because that your faith groweth exceedingly, and the charity of every one of you all toward each other aboundeth; 2 Corinthians 10:15 Not boasting of things without our measure, that is, of other men's labours; but having hope, when your faith is increased, that we shall be enlarged by you according to our rule abundantly,

[166] Mark 5:34 And he said unto her, Daughter, thy faith hath made thee whole; go in peace, and be whole of thy plague.

[167] Mark 5:36 As soon as Jesus heard the word that was spoken, he saith unto the ruler of the synagogue, Be not afraid, only believe.

[168] Mark 10:52 And Jesus said unto him, Go thy way; thy faith hath made thee whole. And immediately he received his sight, and followed Jesus in the way.

[169] Mark 4:40 And he said unto them, Why are ye so fearful? how is it that ye have no faith?

[170] Mark 6:5-6 And he could there do no mighty work, save that he laid his hands upon a few sick folk, and healed them. And he marvelled because of their unbelief. And he went round about the villages, teaching.).

[171] Romans 10:6-8 But the righteousness which is of faith speaketh on this wise, Say not in thine heart, Who shall ascend into heaven? that is, to bring Christ down from above: Or, Who shall descend into the deep? that is, to bring up Christ again from the dead. But what saith it? The word is nigh thee, even in thy mouth, and in thy heart: that is, the word of faith, which we preach; Galatians 3:5 He therefore that ministereth to you the Spirit, and worketh miracles among you, doeth he it by the works of the law, or by the hearing of faith?; 14 That the blessing of Abraham might come on the Gentiles through Jesus Christ; that we might receive the promise of the Spirit through faith; 1 Corinthians 2:4-5 And my speech and my preaching was not with enticing words of man's wisdom, but in demonstration of the Spirit and of power: That your faith should not stand in the wisdom of men, but in the power of God.; 1 Thessalonians 1:5-6 For our gospel came not unto you in word only, but also in power, and in the Holy Ghost, and in much assurance; as ye know what manner of men we were among you for your sake. And ye became followers of us, and of the Lord, having received the word in much affliction, with joy of the Holy Ghost:

[172] 2 Corinthians 4:7 But we have this treasure in earthen vessels, that the excellency of the power may be of God, and not of us.

[173] Ephesians 6:17 And take the helmet of salvation, and the sword of the Spirit, which is the word of God; 1 John 2:27 But the anointing which ye have received of him abideth in you, and ye need not that any man teach you: but as the same anointing teacheth you of all things, and is truth, and is no lie, and even as it hath taught you, ye shall abide in him; Hebrews 8:10-11 For this is the covenant that I will make with the house of Israel after those days, saith the Lord; I will put my laws into their mind, and write them in their hearts: and I will be to them a God, and they shall be to me a people: And they shall not teach every man his neighbour, and every man his brother, saying, Know the Lord: for all shall know me, from the least to the greatest; 2 Corinthians 3:3 Forasmuch as ye are manifestly declared to be the epistle of Christ ministered by us, written not with ink, but with the Spirit of the living God; not in tables of stone, but in fleshy tables of the heart; Ephesians 1:3 Blessed be the God and Father of our Lord Jesus Christ, who hath blessed us with all spiritual blessings in heavenly places in Christ.

[174] 2 Corinthians 13:3 Since ye seek a proof of Christ speaking in me, which to you-ward is not weak, but is mighty in you; 1Th 2:13 For this cause also thank we God without ceasing, because, when ye received the word of God which ye heard of us, ye received it not as the word of men, but as it is in truth, the word of God, which effectually worketh also in you that believe; 1 Peter 1:11 Searching what, or what manner of time the Spirit of Christ which was in them did signify, when it testified beforehand the sufferings of Christ, and the glory that should follow.

[175] Hebrews 6:12 That ye be not slothful, but followers of them who through faith and patience inherit the promises.; Mark 11:23 For verily I say unto you, That whosoever shall say unto this mountain, Be thou removed, and be thou cast into the sea; and shall not doubt in his heart, but shall believe that those things which he saith shall come to pass; he shall have whatsoever he saith.

[176] *Exodus 19:19 And when the voice of the trumpet sounded long, and waxed louder and louder, Moses spake, and God answered him by a voice; Ex 20:19 And they said unto Moses, Speak thou with us, and we will hear: but let not God speak with us, lest we die.*

[177] *Deuteronomy 30:13-14 Neither is it beyond the sea, that thou shouldest say, Who shall go over the sea for us, and bring it unto us, that we may hear it, and do it? But the word is very nigh unto thee, in thy mouth, and in thy heart, that thou mayest do it;*

[178] *Acts 20:32 And now, brethren, I commend you to God, and to the word of his grace, which is able to build you up, and to give you an inheritance among all them which are sanctified.*

[179] *Psalms 33:6; By the word of the LORD were the heavens made; and all the host of them by the breath of his mouth; Hebrews 11:3 Through faith we understand that the worlds were framed by the word of God, so that things which are seen were not made of things which do appear.*

[180] *1 Peter 3:10 For he that will love life, and see good days, let him refrain his tongue from evil, and his lips that they speak no guile; Psalms 34:13 Keep thy tongue from evil, and thy lips from speaking guile.*

[181] *Psalms 84:11 For the LORD God is a sun and shield: the LORD will give grace and glory: no good thing will he withhold from them that walk uprightly; Mt 6:33 But seek ye first the kingdom of God, and his righteousness; and all these things shall be added unto you.*

[182] *Isaiah 40:30-31 Even the youths shall faint and be weary, and the young men shall utterly fall: But they that wait upon the LORD shall renew their strength; they shall mount up with wings as eagles; they shall run, and not be weary; and they*

shall walk, and not faint; Galatians 6:9 And let us not be weary in well doing: for in due season we shall reap, if we faint not.

[183] Psalms 19:14 Let the words of my mouth, and the meditation of my heart, be acceptable in thy sight, O LORD, my strength, and my redeemer.

[184] Matthew 12:37 For by thy words thou shalt be justified, and by thy words thou shalt be condemned; Proverbs 13:3 He that keepeth his mouth keepeth his life: but he that openeth wide his lips shall have destruction.

[185] Hebrews 11:8 By faith Abraham, when he was called to go out into a place which he should after receive for an inheritance, obeyed; and he went out, not knowing whither he went.

[186] Hebrews 10:23 Let us hold fast the profession of our faith without wavering; (for he is faithful that promised;); 11:11 Through faith also Sara herself received strength to conceive seed, and was delivered of a child when she was past age, because she judged him faithful who had promised; 2 Corinthians 1:20 For all the promises of God in him are yea, and in him Amen, unto the glory of God by us.

[187] Romans 4:20-21 He staggered not at the promise of God through unbelief; but was strong in faith, giving glory to God; And being fully persuaded that, what he had promised, he was able also to perform.

[188] Galatians 5:22-23 But the fruit of the Spirit is love, joy, peace, longsuffering, gentleness, goodness, faith, Meekness, temperance: against such there is no law; 1 Corinthians 12:8-9 For to one is given by the Spirit the word of wisdom; to another the word of knowledge by the same Spirit; To another faith by the same Spirit; to another the gifts of healing by the same Spirit;; Acts 4:31 And when they had prayed, the place was shaken where they

were assembled together; and they were all filled with the Holy Ghost, and they spake the word of God with boldness.; Jeremiah 17:5-6 Thus saith the LORD; Cursed be the man that trusteth in man, and maketh flesh his arm, and whose heart departeth from the LORD. For he shall be like the heath in the desert, and shall not see when good cometh; but shall inhabit the parched places in the wilderness, in a salt land and not inhabited.

[189] Romans 10:14 How then shall they call on him in whom they have not believed? and how shall they believe in him of whom they have not heard? and how shall they hear without a preacher?

[190] Isaiah 65:16 That he who blesseth himself in the earth shall bless himself in the God of truth; and he that sweareth in the earth shall swear by the God of truth; because the former troubles are forgotten, and because they are hid from mine eyes; Revelation 3:14 And unto the angel of the church of the Laodiceans write; These things saith the Amen, the faithful and true witness, the beginning of the creation of God; 2 Corinthians 1:20 For all the promises of God in him are yea, and in him Amen, unto the glory of God by us.

[191] Romans 10:16 But they have not all obeyed the gospel. For Esaias saith, Lord, who hath believed our report?; Isaiah 53:1 Who hath believed our report? and to whom is the arm of the LORD revealed?